England

by Terry Marsh

Terry Marsh is a travel writer
specialising in the countryside
of Britain. He contributes regularly
to newspapers and magazines, and has
written over 30 books.

*Above: delightful timber-framed houses in
Saffron Walden*

AA Publishing

Above: *punting on the River Cherwell in Oxford*

Written by Terry Marsh

First published 2001
Reprinted 2004. Information updated and verified.

© Automobile Association Developments Limited 2004

Published by AA Publishing, a trading name of Automobile Association Developments Limited, whose registered office is Millstream, Maidenhead Road, Windsor, Berkshire SL4 5GD. Registered number 1878835.

Mapping produced by the Cartograhic Department of Automobile Association Developments Limited.

A CIP catalogue record for this book is available from the British Library.

Find out more about AA Publishing and the wide range of travel publications and services the AA provides by visiting our web site at www.theAA.com

A01641

Colour separation: Chroma Graphics (Overseas) Pte Ltd, Singapore
Printed and bound in Italy by Printer Trento S.r.l

Contents

About this Book

KEY TO SYMBOLS

➕ map reference to the maps found in the What to See section

✉ address or location

☎ telephone number

🕐 opening times

🍴 restaurant or café on premises or near by

Ⓐ nearest underground train station

🚌 nearest bus/tram route

🚃 nearest overground train station

⛴ ferry crossings and boat excursions

ℹ tourist information

♿ facilities for visitors with disabilities

✋ admission charge

↔ other places of interest near by

❓ other practical information

▶ indicates the page where you will find a fuller description

✈ travel by air

This book is divided into five sections to cover the most important aspects of your visit to England.

Viewing England pages 5–14
An introduction to England by the author.
England's Features
Essence of England
The Shaping of England
Peace and Quiet
England's Famous

Top Ten pages 15–26
The author's choice of the Top Ten places to see in England, listed in alphabetical order, each with practical information.

What to See pages 27–90
The five main areas of England, each with its own brief introduction and an alphabetical listing of the main attractions.
Practical information
Snippets of 'Did you know…' information
3 suggested walks and two drives
2 features

Where To... pages 91–116
Detailed listings of the best places to eat, stay, shop, take the children and be entertained.

Practical Matters pages 117–24
A highly visual section containing essential travel information.

Maps
All map references are to the individual maps found in the What to See section of this guide.
For example, Castle Howard has the reference ➕ 41C2 – indicating the page on which the map is located and the grid square in which the stately home is to be found. A list of the maps that have been used in this travel guide can be found in the index.

Prices
Where appropriate, an indication of the cost of an establishment is given by £ signs:
£££ denotes higher prices, **££** denotes average prices, while **£** denotes lower charges.

Star Ratings
Most of the places described in this book have been given a separate rating:
😊😊😊   Do not miss
😊😊   Highly recommended
😊   Worth seeing

Viewing
England

Above: Ironbridge and the River Severn
Below: open-topped buses are a splendid, if breezy, way to see London

Terry Marsh's England

For many visitors it is hard to comprehend the variety England has to offer, from its charming country villages to the magnificent monuments of its great cities; a place of extremes but also a place that seems very much homogeneous and united. It is tempting, being born and raised in the North of England, to eulogise exclusively about the North, its fantastic scenery, its wealth of historical associations, its sense of camaraderie and humour. But that would be to render the South of England a grave disservice, for this is a richly varied country and, if I'm being honest rather than parochial, the beauties and attractions of the South are just as great and characteristic of this immensely fascinating country.

Today England is a world leader in art, music and fashion. Politically and economically it is still a major player, as a part of the United Kingdom. There is a great feeling of openness, of a willingness to share England's heritage, whatever form it takes, with visitors and local people alike.

But England is also very European, in spite of the political bickering that goes on. Gone is the arrogance of imperialism; instead there is a recognition that England is one among many on the world's stage, with a role for everyone. It is a more worldly, more enterprising place that above all has a developing pride in its history and its place in the world.

Above: *a restored steam engine on the Severn Valley Railway*

Seeing England
You can charge around on well-organised sightseeing tours, cramming in the sights, listening to the patter and getting a taste of what your guide would have you believe England is about. Or you can step off this merry-go-round, and explore the cities, towns and villages on foot with nothing more than a locally produced leaflet to set you on your way. This is by far the best way to discover what makes England tick.

Right: *the beautiful Aysgarth Falls in Wensleydale*

England's Features

The Country

- England is the largest political division of the United Kingdom of Great Britain and Northern Ireland.
- It is a highly industrialised and agriculturally developed country, densely populated and rich in history.
- London, the capital, is also by far England's largest city, with over 7 million inhabitants.
- Birmingham in central England, the next largest city, has around a million inhabitants.

Below: *stone-built farms and hillscapes patterned by drystone walls are typical of the Yorkshire Dales' landscape*

- Northern England boasts a clutch of cities with around 500,000 inhabitants, including Leeds, Manchester, Liverpool, Bradford, Sheffield and Newcastle. In the southwest Bristol and Plymouth are the largest centres of population.

The Economy

- England's most important exports are oil, gas, technology and financial services.
- 50 years ago the most important exports were coal, iron, steel, shipbuilding, textiles and pottery.

A Few Facts and Figures

Area: 50,331sq miles/130,357sq km
Currency: pound (£) sterling
Population approx 50,000,000 in 2000
Language: English, with many varied dialects and several hundred minority languages

The People
England today is a multiracial nation where traditional notions of social class are less important than they once were. There is still an aristocracy, though its governing privileges in the House of Lords were drastically reduced in 1999. Most people like to think of themselves as 'middle class' these days.

Essence of England

Above: *browsing in second-hand bookshops can become addictive*

England really is a green and pleasant land, a place of rolling landscapes and scenery that can make your heart ache. But it's also a varied and very cosmopolitan country, and offers so much that it is almost folly to try to cram everything into one visit (you simply won't). The secret is not to be too hasty. Linger, perhaps longer than you intended, whenever a particular place captures your imagination. Be flexible, change your plans as you go along, and be prepared to spend time exploring street markets or car boot sales, go for a walk in a town park, or simply enjoy a pint of beer at the local pub.

Below: *Bibury – William Morris's 'most beautiful Cotswold village'*

THE 10 ESSENTIALS

If you only have a short time to visit England, or would like to get a really complete picture of the country, here are the essentials:

• **Take a ride in a London cab** – ask the cabbie to show you as many of the sights of London as he can in an hour. Avoid rush hours and try fixing a charge first.
• **Try fish and chips** – not really the English staple diet, but very filling.
• **Visit a stately home** – you'll find them all over the country, but allow enough time to see everything.
• **Explore the Lake District** – there is so much beautiful countryside in England, but the Lake District crams a lot in a small space (➤ 20–1).
• **Visit a cathedral** – every one is an architectural marvel, and a peaceful place where you can slow things down for a while.
• **Try real ale** or cider, particualarly in a traditional English pub.

• **Visit an industrial museum** – there are many around the country, but the Ironbridge Gorge (➤ 59) in Shropshire is looked on as the cradle of the Industrial Revolution.
• **Go shopping in a street market** – markets are a

traditional feature of many English towns. The modern versions are the car boot sales which are usually advertised on the approach to towns and villages.
• **Walk a town trail** – one of the best ways of getting to know a place: leaflets are available at the local tourist information centre.
• **Visit a village fête or agricultural show** – always a fascinating day out, with cattle shows, dog trials, folk dancing, wrestling, cookery competitions, craft displays and something for all the family.

Left: *take a ride in a London cab*

Below: *a smiling welcome in a traditional pub, the Green Dragon in Horsham*

Left: *battered fish, chips and mushy peas – England's own fastfood*

9

The Shaping of England

6500 BC
England is cut off from mainland Europe when rising sea-levels flood the Straits of Dover.

3200–2000 BC
Stonehenge and other great neolithic monuments are built.

55–54 BC
Julius Caesar makes expeditions to England

AD 43
The Roman Emperor Claudius invades Britain.

50
Romans build *Londinium*, later to become London.

140
Roman power extends into Scotland before being stabilised behind Hadrian's Wall in 163.

410
The Romans withdraw, Germanic tribes – Angles, Saxons and Jutes – begin to colonise England.

Below: *Stonehenge is the most famous prehistoric monument in Britain*

Right: *the Black Death killed thousands in 1348*

663
Anglo-Saxons reject the Celtic church in favour of Roman Christianity.

865–78
Viking/Danish armies occupy England, taking York in 867 and London in 872. In 878 Alfred defeats the Danes, with an English army.

973
Coronation of Edgar, first king of England, in Bath.

1016
The Dane Cnut heads a North Sea kingdom which includes England, Denmark, western Sweden and Norway.

1066
The Norman Conquest. William, Duke of Normandy, defeats Harold near Hastings, and is crowned at Westminster Abbey.

1086
William orders the Domesday Survey, recording the details of every English village.

1215
King John assents to the Magna Carta, asserting that the monarch is not above the law.

1337
Beginning of the 'Hundred Years War' with France.

1348–50
The Black Death sweeps across England. In some areas up to 50 per cent of the population dies.

1509
Henry VIII crowned. During his reign the monasteries are dissolved, Wales is incorporated into the English state and the Church of England is established.

1642–9
The English Civil War, between parliament and Charles I, ends with his execution.

1649–53
The Commonwealth under Oliver Cromwell. The Monarchy is abolished. Tea is introduced.

1660
The restoration of the Monarchy. Charles II accedes to the throne.

1707
Act of Union with Scotland. English ports such as Bristol and Liverpool prospering through the slave trade.

19th century
Industrial expansion transforms England from a rural to an urban society. The British Empire extends to over 3.5 million square miles.

1815
The Battle of Waterloo. Napoleon is defeated by the Duke of Wellington.

1837
Victoria becomes queen; her reign lasts until 1901.

1914–18
World War I ends an unprecedented period of imperial expansion and cultural development.

1918
Women vote for the first time in an election.

1924
First Labour government.

1939–45
World War II; Churchill becomes prime minister; Battle of Britain and defeat of Germany.

1945
Churchill's Conservatives lose election to Labour Party who nationalise transport, the coal mines and other industries and establish a welfare state.

1960s
English pop music, from the Beatles to the Rolling Stones, achieves global fame. England beats Germany in the football World Cup final.

1973
Britain enters the European Union.

1979
Margaret Thatcher becomes Britain's first woman prime minister.

1994
Channel rail tunnel links London and Paris.

1997
Tony Blair's Labour Party ends 18 years of Conservative rule.

1999
Government in Westminster devolves powers to assemblies in Wales, Scotland and Northern Ireland.

2002
Queen Elizabeth II celebrates her Golden Jubilee.

The Battle of Waterloo

Peace & Quiet

Above: the wild and rugged Cheviot Hills are a popular walking area

Travel can be a wearisome business at times, so it's good to know that it is never difficult to escape the crowds. In England, 11 National Parks offer almost 5,000sq miles (13,000sq km) of countryside, protected for their scenic and recreational value. There are also more than 40 designated Areas of Outstanding Natural Beauty (AONB), with a similar protected status. Spread across the English countryside is a massive network of thousands of miles of footpaths, bridleways (open to horses and cyclists) and byways. There are ten National Trails (long-distance paths) and scores of lesser routes with good signposting and supporting literature.

Most towns and cities have formal parks in or near their centres, while in the surrounding areas you'll find country parks, where there is a less formal environment, and a greater chance of seeing some wildlife. Among the best scenic areas not mentioned elsewhere in this book, try seeking out the following.

The Cheviot Hills

By international standards the Cheviots, at the northern end of the Pennines, are minor hills; a wild and rugged expanse of upland, rising to little more than 2,600ft (792m). Rocky outcrops are few, and the highest ground is a peaty morass, but here you can walk for miles without meeting another soul. The most visited parts surround the northern end of the Pennine Way National Trail.

Forest of Bowland

In the north of Lancashire you'll find the moorland expanse of the Forest of Bowland and Pendle AONB, a place where charming, isolated farmsteads and villages bury themselves among the folds of the heather and bracken covered hills. This is perfect walking country and there is a well-developed local ranger service.

The Peak District

In spite of being the world's second most visited national park (the first is Mount Fuji in Japan), the Peak District still hides a few places where visitors can enjoy quiet and solitude. In the southern and central part of the National Park – the White Peak – the limestone creates a bright, scenically invigorating landscape of green meadows and homely villages, cut by lovely dales and gorges like Dovedale, Monsal Dale and Lathkill Dale (► 56). To the north and west, the Dark Peak is dominated by the sombre colours of gritstone, creating dramatic rock profiles and stark scenery. The area is rich in walking and cycling trails and the Pennine Way National Trail begins on the peaty upland plateaux of Kinder and Bleaklow.

The Shropshire Hills

Lying between the Wyre Forest and the Welsh border, the Shropshire Hills are a series of parallel ridges of weathered, ancient rock, up to 1,000 million years old. Most notable among these hills is the Long Mynd, a broad moorland plateau rising to its highest point at Pole Bank (1,696ft/517m), from where there is an unobstructed view of the Malvern Hills, the Cotswolds (► 17), Snowdonia in North Wales and the Brecon Beacons in South Wales. To the west a desolate, rock-strewn heather and bilberry moorland, crowned with hard, sandstone crags known as the Stiperstones, is a national nature reserve and an important upland habitat for wildlife.

Below: *Dovedale, in Derbyshire's White Peak, has long been recognised for its sylvan beauty*

England's Famous

Above: *Margaret Thatcher, Britain's first woman prime minister*

Margaret Thatcher (1925-)

From the moment she entered 10 Downing Street in 1979, as the new Conservative Prime Minister, this former research chemist from Grantham in Lincolnshire transformed British politics and culture. Skilfully combining populist rhetoric with the philosophy of the free market, she set about dismantling the institutions which had underpinned the state since 1945. Her period of office included a war with Argentina over the Falkland Islands, the collapse of the Soviet Union and, at home, political strife and popular unrest. Ousted in 1990, as Baroness Thatcher of Kesteven she continues to exert influence from the sidelines, writing memoirs and lecturing around the world.

Charles Robert Darwin (1809-82)

English naturalist, born in Shrewsbury, and the originator (with Alfred Russel Wallace) of the theory of evolution by natural selection. He was educated at Shrewsbury grammar school, studied medicine at Edinburgh, and then, intending to enter the Church, went to Christ's College, Cambridge, in 1828. Later, however, he travelled widely, and this provided him with an intimate knowledge of the flora, fauna and geology of many lands.

The Beatles
The four-piece Beatles – John Lennon, Paul McCartney, George Harrison and Ringo Starr – transformed the face of popular music and were the the first English band to challenge the US dominance of rock and roll music. Not everyone shared the popular view of 'The Fab Four'. When they received MBEs in 1965, disgruntled colonels sent their medals back to the Queen. But their popularity was otherwise universal, songs such as *Yesterday* and *Let it be* have become known throughout the world, and they continue to influence the world of pop music long after their break-up in 1970.

William Shakespeare (1564–1616)

Widely regarded as the most outstanding writer in the English language, the creator of *Romeo and Juliet*, *Hamlet* and *A Midsummer Night's Dream*, was a playwright, poet, actor, joint manager of a London acting company and part owner of one of its theatres. Born in Stratford-upon-Avon (➤ 63) in Warwickshire, he lived partly in Stratford and partly in London.

Sir Paul McCartney (1942–)

Rock singer, world-acclaimed songwriter and bass guitarist in the Beatles. Paul McCartney was later leader of the pop group Wings, in which his US-born wife, Linda (1942–1998) also performed. McCartney formed an irrepressible songwriting partnership with John Lennon (1940–80), a founder member of the Beatles. With composer Carl Davis, he turned to classical music, composing the *Liverpool Oratorio* in 1991, and later produced *Standing Stones*, which received critical acclaim in the USA. He was knighted in 1997.

Top Ten

Above: *the Rose Window, York Minster*
Right: *the white rose of Yorkshire displayed on a City of York sign*

15

1
Bath

✠ 67E3

ℹ Abbey Chambers,
☎ 01225 477101;
www.visitbath.co.uk

Roman Baths Museum

✉ Pump Room, Abbey Church Yard

☎ 01225 477785

🕐 Mar–Jun, Sep–Oct, daily 9–5; Jul, Aug, 9–9; rest of year 9.30–4.30

✋ Expensive

Museum of Costume

✉ Bennett Street

☎ 01225 477789

🕐 Daily 10–5

✋ Moderate

American Museum

✉ Claverton Manor

☎ 01225 460503

✋ Moderate

Above: *the Gorgon's Head, Roman Baths*
Below: *the sweeping Royal Crescent*

Bath is best known for its sweeping crescents of Georgian townhouses and the remains of its Roman baths, now restored at the centre of the city.

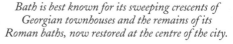

The Romans built a temple to the local water goddess Sulis here, and the first Bath spa (Aqua Sulis) was founded. The **Roman remains** are among the most important in Europe, and heavily visited, being in the centre of town. Little survives from the Saxon and medieval towns which followed, though they were obviously of some importance. Edgar was crowned first king of all England here in 973.

The Abbey church, completed in 1499, stands across an enclosed square and contains some splendid vaulting. Aside from a heavily restored section of the old city walls, the rest of Bath is dominated by the changes wrought by leisure developers in the middle of the 18th century. Bath was then reinvented as the spa playground of the century's nouveaux riches. The Royal Crescent, Paragon, Circus and Lansdown Crescent were all magnificent streets, built to accommodate the influx of wealthy pleasure-seekers, who came for the waters and the social scene. A walk today across Robert Adam's Pulteney Bridge to the fascinating Holburne Museum of Art reveals the scale of this Georgian re-building. Walking is the best way to see the city, as the traffic in its baffling one-way system can feel chaotic, but there are a number of open-top bus tours which take in the less accessible quarters which spread up the steep hillsides.

Other sights you must seek out include the world-famous **Museum of Costume** housed in the Assembly Rooms, Cross Bath, Queen Square and Victoria Park, a green thoroughfare to the suburb of Weston. Within a few miles of the centre, Prior Park is a restored landscape garden from the city's heyday. Designed by Ralph Allen and Capability Brown, it has tremendous views. The award-winning **American Museum of Decorative Art** is also near by at Claverton Manor.

2
Cotswolds

The warmth of the honey-coloured stone villages and the rich green landscape confirm the Cotswolds as one of England's most beautiful areas.

The Cotswolds, a range of hills divided into two by the River Chum, represent the quintessential English landscape; rolling green hills, mellow-coloured farms, and picturesque towns and villages. They form an Area of Outstanding Natural Beauty covering 790sq miles (2,038sq km), and spanning six counties from Bath in the south to Edge Hill in the north.

The great parish churches and inns demonstrate the prosperity of the area which began in the late Middle Ages. Sheep farming underpinned this wealth and made a huge impact on the landscape as the Cotswolds became rich on wool and cloth. Chipping Camden, Northleach and Cirencester contain good examples of 'wool churches', heavily adorned with gargoyles.

The village of Broadway acts as a gateway to the region, with tourist shops and tearooms abounding. Bourton-on-the-Water is another honeypot, with the River Windrush running pleasantly through its centre. Upper and Lower Slaughter attract visitors as much for their peculiar names as their chocolate-box looks. You can get a better feel for the Cotswolds' charm in less-visited gems such as Stanton, Snowshill or Bibury. Arlington Row, a delightful terrace of former weavers' cottages in Bibury best epitomises Cotswold village character, and the nearby **Mill** houses an excellent folk museum.

🔲 67E4

Arlington Mill Museum

☎ 01285 740368

🕐 Mar–Oct, daily, 10–6; Nov–Feb, Mon–Fri, 10–5, Sat–Sun, 10–5.30

✋ Cheap

♿ None

ℹ️ There is no one tourist organisation for the whole region. It's a question of contacting the individual tourist offices, but start with Cheltenham (☎ 01242 522878; www. visitcheltenham.gov.uk).

Below: *Snowshill is pronounced 'Snossel' by the locals*

3
Exmoor

✚ 66C3

✉ Exmoor National Park, Fore Street, Dulverton, Somerset TA22 9EX

☎ 01398 323665; www.visit-exmoor.info

Sweeping heather moors are split by wooded coombs which tumble into the sea in this National Park on the Somerset/Devon border.

Within the 265sq miles (68,632ha) of Exmoor lie extensive heath and grass moors, woodlands and plantations, a high moorland plateau and steep-sided valleys, cultivated farmland and rough grazing, as well as splendid sea cliffs, features that have an important influence on the way the area is run.

The national park borders the Bristol Channel and enjoys something of a refreshing maritime climate. It reaches its highest point on Dunkery Beacon, at 1,702ft (519m) with breathtaking views of the valleys of the Barle, the Exe and the East and West Lyn rivers.

At the northern edge of the Park, where it edges the Bristol Channel, the twin towns of Lynton and Lynmouth are linked by a 19th-century water-powered cliff railway. The lower town, at the mouth of the two Lyn rivers, was famously devastated by a flood in 1953. The upper town boasts fine views and leads to the spectacular dry Valley of the Rocks, running parallell with the dramatic 500ft (150m) coastal cliffs. Nearby Watersmeet is a popular beauty spot deep in a tree-lined ravine where Hoar Oak Water joins the East Lyn River. This is superb walking country, and best visited after rain, when the rivers are full of life and the waterfalls spectacular.

For many people, however, Exmoor is synonymous with R D Blackmore's novel, *Lorna Doone*, a tale of thwarted love, villains and passion set amid the brooding moors, and published in 1869. Henry Williamson's classic wildlife story, *Tarka the Otter*, was also inspired by the author's time on Exmoor. The largest wildlife in the area is the red deer, the stag's antlers making up the National Park logo.

Above: *the view from Dunkery Beacon, the highest point of Exmoor*

Right: *the image of a red deer features in the logo for Exmoor National Park*

4
Housesteads, Hadrian's Wall

The purpose of the great Roman wall was 'to separate the Romans from the Barbarians' – 'qui barbaros Romanosque divideret…'

One of a series of Roman boundary fortifications built right across northern Europe, Hadrian's Wall stretches for 73 miles (117km) between Wallsend, on the east coast near Newcastle upon Tyne, to Bowness-on-Solway in Cumbria on the west coast. Begun in AD 122, it took six years to complete and is 10ft (3m) thick in places. The walkway which ran along the top was sometimes as high as 12ft (3.5m) above the ground.

The wall was built to protect Roman Britain from raiding Picts from what is now Scotland, and the most dramatic sections still run close to the Anglo-Scottish border. Abandoned in 383, much of the stone from the wall was used in local buildings, but enough remains to give a vivid picture of a Roman frontier province. A World Heritage Site, there are many museums and interpretive centres along the wall that portray life in Roman times, notably at Birdoswald, Once Brewed, Vindolanda and Chesters, but the best is the **Housesteads Fort and Museum**. Known to the Romans as Vercovicium, Housesteads is the most complete Roman fort in Britain, and occupies a spectacular position with commanding views across the bleak Northumbrian countryside. It was garrisoned by about 1,000 soldiers and the museum recreates aspects of their life as well as explaining the natural history of the region. A new National Trail is being developed which will follow the course of the wall and will open for walkers in 2002.

 40B4

The Manor Office, Hallgate, Hexham NE46 1XD ☎ 01434 652220; www.hadrians-wall.org.uk

Housesteads Fort and Museum

✉ Housesteads

☎ 01434 344363

🕐 Apr–Sep daily 10–6; Oct–Mar 10–4. Closed 24–26 Dec, 1 Jan

♿ None

 Moderate

Below: *take a walk along Hadrian's Wall, built to protect Roman Britain from the Barbarians to the north*

5
Lake District

Few places in England have the richly varied landscape of the Lake District; fewer still its wealth of local history and legends.

40A3

ℹ️ Lake District National Park Authority, Murley Moss, Oxenholme Road, Kendal, Cumbria LA9 7RL ☎ 01539 724555; www.lake-district.gov.uk

Lake District Visitor Centre

✉️ Brockhole (on A591 between Windermere and Ambleside)

☎️ 015394 46601

🌐 Apr–Nov daily 10–5; grounds and gardens, all year daily

♿ Free; parking £4 per day

Above: *the Wordsworths loved beautiful Rydal Water and skated there in winter*

The Lake District, which forms part of Cumbria in north-west England, is acknowledged nationally and internationally as a special place of landscape beauty, drawing visitors from all over the world. Covering 885sq miles (2,292sq km) this is the largest and most spectacular of England's national parks. It contains England's biggest lakes and mountains, in a combination that is never less than exhilarating. Windermere is England's longest lake (10½ miles/17km from Waterhead to Lakeside), Wastwater its deepest (258ft/79m) and Scafell Pike its highest mountain at 3,210ft/978m. Here you'll also find England's steepest roads (Hardknott Pass is 33 per cent), its smallest church (St Olaf's in Wasdale), its only nesting golden eagles (above Haweswater), and, at Santon Bridge on the western fringe, England's biggest liar, who is determined to win an annual competition.

The Lake District is basically a system of valleys (or 'dales') radiating from a central core of mountains, known as 'fells' (from the Norse settlers' 'fjall'). This is prime walking country and thousands flock to the popular summits, such as Scafell Pike, Helvellyn, Skiddaw and Great Gable. Despite their modest altitude, the weather can be very severe here and care should be taken. But there are over 1,500 miles (2,414km) of footpaths covering all types of terrain, from lakesides to quiet forests and exhilarating open moors, ensuring there is some walking to suit everyone. There are also plenty of guidebooks to help you find your way and guided walks are available in the main walkers' centres such as Coniston and Keswick.

Of the principal tourist centres, Windermere (town), Bowness and Kendal attract thousands of daytrippers and are easily accessible by road and rail. Many make for the **Visitor Centre** at Brockhole. Keswick, in the north, nestles amid towering fells beside Derwent Water and has a seemingly limitless development of outdoor clothing shops. Ambleside, at the head of Windermere (lake), in the south, plays a similar role. Grasmere, with nearby Rydal, is between the two and famously associated with the poet William Wordsworth, a Cumbrian who did much of his best work while living here.

Wordsworth was one of a group of 'Lakes Poets' with Coleridge, Southey and de Quincey. They are often credited with popularising the Lake District as a tourist attraction in the late 18th and early 19th centuries. The Victorian intellectual and critic John Ruskin spent the last years of his life at Brantwood on the shores of Coniston Water. Hugh Walpole, Richard Adams and Arthur Ransome all used the unique landscape to good effect in their work. Beatrix Potter, whose children's books such as *Peter Rabbit* were based on her observations of family and wildlife at her home at Near Sawrey, left her considerable Lake District estate to the National Trust. Her home is now a popular museum.

To escape the crowds in this heavily visited region, you should make for the fringes of the national park. Wasdale and Eskdale in the west, and Mardale and Swindale in the east, are quieter valleys without the occasional summer traffic problems which curse the centre of the park. But on most days, even the popular valleys of Langdale, Buttermere and Borrowdale are surprisingly peaceful. The only sounds which punctuate the silence will be the forlorn bleating of the local Herdwick sheep and the roar of the occasional practising military jet.

Below: *take a trip on an Ullswater steamer, here the* Lady of the Lake

Below: *Derwent Water and the distant bulk of Blencathra, a landscape to make your heart ache*

6
Oxford

55C1

The Old School, Gloucester Green ☎ 01865 726871 🕐 Mon–Sat 9:30–5; Sun May–Oct 10–3:30

🍴 Try one of the sandwich bars in the covered market

Ashmolean Museum

✉ Beaumont Street

☎ 01865 278000; www.ashmol.ox.ac.uk

🕐 Tue–Sat 10–5, Sun 2–5. Closed 1 Jan, Good Fri–Easter Sun, 3 days early Sep, 24–28 Dec

🍴 Digby Trout Restaurant (££)

♿ Excellent

🖐 Free

❓ Guided tours

Bodleian Library

✉ Broad Street

☎ 01865 277180; www.bodley.ox.ac.uk

🕐 Mon–Fri 9–5 (closing times can vary), Sat 9–1. Closed Xmas and Easter

🖐 Cheap

❓ Guided tours

Above: *outstanding architecture dominates the Oxford scene, where 'town' and 'gown' coexist uneasily*

Oxford is an important industrial and commercial centre, dominated both historically and physically by its university.

Modern Oxford sprawls eastwards and includes car plants and technology industries as well as the more predictable publishing houses and English language schools within its city limits. The University's colleges, of which there are 36, are large and complex institutions and exert considerable influence, though they do not entirely monopolise city life. Oxford coexists with its student population rather less comfortably than might be supposed, a state of mild tension between 'town' and 'gown'.

It is the architecture of the colleges which first impresses the visitor. There are masterpieces from many periods, from the early Gothic of Merton College to the experimental modernism of St Catherine's. The location of the college buildings in the city centre gives Oxford a truly historic feel. The centre is surrounded by meadows and parkland, preserved by the various colleges, and these too, with their cyclists, punters and rowers, add to the ambience of gentility. There has been educational influence in the city since at least 1167 when students expelled from Paris settled here under the patronage of Henry II. The colleges, with their quadrangles, refectories and chapels, still reflect the structures of the religious houses upon which they were founded.

Of outstanding interest is the **Ashmolean Museum**, England's oldest public museum, founded in 1683. It houses the University's enormous collections of art and antiquities. On the corner of Broad Street you'll find the **Bodleian Library** and the Sheldonian Theatre, in a quarter of 17th-century buildings which seems designed to meet the visitor's expectations of this venerable city.

7
Stonehenge

The great stone circle at Stonehenge is one of the wonders of the world, as old as many of the temples and pyramids of Egypt.

Stonehenge (from the Old English 'hanging stones') is 2 miles (3km) west of Amesbury in Wiltshire, and one of the best-known archaeological sites in the world. It is not, as might be supposed, an isolated monument. In reality, the stones form only a part of an extensive prehistoric landscape filled with the remains of ceremonial and domestic structures.

What you see today is the last in a series of monuments erected in several stages between 3000 and 1600 BC. Each is circular in form and aligned along the rising of the sun at the midsummer solstice, though many of the structures are incomplete.

Archaeologists still debate whether Stonehenge was a place of ritual sacrifice and sun worship, some kind of astronomical calculator, or a royal palace. But for thousands of years it was an important focal point within a ceremonial landscape. The structure also represents a massive investment in time and human resources. Enormous effort was needed to transport the stones, some weighing up to 40 tons, from sites tens or hundreds of miles away, notably from Preseli in Wales, from where they must have been dragged or floated on rafts.

Stonehenge is now a UNESCO World Heritage Site, and although conflict has arisen, between modern druids, new-age travellers and the police, there is no doubt that the conservation of this outstanding site has been taken very seriously. There are recommended walks exploring the surrounding downland of Salisbury Plain and an archaeological leaflet available from the shop to help you interpret this ancient landscape.

✚ 67E3

✉ near Amesbury, Wiltshire

☎ 01980 624715 24-hour information line; www.stonehengemasterplan.org.uk

🕐 Mid-Mar to Jun, Sep to mid-Oct daily 9.30–6; Jun–Sep 9–7; mid to late Oct 9.30–5; late Oct to mid-Mar 9.30–4. Closed 24–26 Dec and 1 Jan

🍴 Stonehenge Kitchen (£–££)

♿ Good

✋ Moderate

❓ Self-guided audio tours

Stonehenge: a place of sacrifice, a calculator or a royal palace?

8
Tower of London

See the Crown Jewels at the Tower of London

Overlooking the Thames, the Tower of London is famous as a place of imprisonment and death; it's also one of England's foremost medieval fortresses.

 31F3

☎ 0870 756 6060; www. tower-of-london-org.uk

🕐 Mar–Oct, Mon–Sat 9–6, Sun 10–6; Nov–Feb, Tue–Sat 9–5, Sun, Mon 10–5. Last admission 1 hour before closing. Closed 1 Jan, 24–26 Dec

🍴 Café (£)

🚇 Tower Hill

🚌 15, 25, 42, 78, 100, D1

🚆 Fenchurch Street (British Rail); Tower Gateway (DLR)

♿ Tower staff are willing to help, but there are inherent problems with old buildings. Phone in advance for advice

✋ Very expensive

❓ Buy tickets in advance from any underground station to avoid waiting at the Tower entrance. Free hour-long tours run about every half hour.

The Tower, not just one tower but a whole castle-full, is one of London's great landmarks. It has been a royal residence, an armoury and the home, as it still is, of the Crown Jewels. The oldest part is the White Tower, begun in 1078. It is surrounded by Tower Green, where the executions of Lady Jane Grey, Anne Boleyn and Catherine Howard took place. Here you'll find two of the Tower's famous ravens, the latest in a long line protected by royal decree. Their wings are clipped to prevent them flying away. Legend claims that should they leave, the Tower and the kingdom will fall.

Walks around the Tower are conducted by Yeoman Warders (Beefeaters), who recount tales of torture and intrigue, and provide a more organised way of experiencing the Tower's history than wandering around by yourself.

The Crown Jewels are housed in the Jewel House, and viewing them, after what may be a long wait in a queue, is rather hurried as visitors are carried along moving walkways that permit only a brief glimpse. Among the dazzling display the Imperial State Crown contains a 317-carat diamond, sapphires, emeralds, rubies and pearls, but the most famous of the diamonds is the Koh-i-Noor, set into a crown made for the Queen Mother in 1937.

In the Bloody Tower are the rooms where the 'Princes in the Tower', the 12-year-old Edward V and his brother Richard, were murdered by Richard III and where Sir Walter Raleigh was held captive for 13 years.

9
York

York is one of the few cities that stills feels medieval. Begun by the Romans in AD 71, it became an important city, which they called Eboracum.

'York' comes from the Scandanavian *Jorvik*, and the **Viking Centre** in Coppergate houses a vivid display of York under their domination. Later, the Normans made York their centre of government, commerce and religion in the north. Pride of place went to the magnificent Minster, which took 250 years to build and was completed and consecrated in 1472. Now one of the city's essential visitor attractions, it contains England's finest collection of medieval stained glass.

During the Middle Ages, York was an important wool-trading centre. On the prosperity of this trade rode the success of other tradespeople, notably goldsmiths, butchers, shoemakers and saddlers, who came to live, and thrived in the city. Many of these lived in Stonegate, Goodramgate and the Shambles, streets which are still very medieval in appearance. The modern shops are still shaped around the plots laid out for the city's development over 1,000 years ago.

The medieval city walls are also largely intact and make an interesting circular walk of around 2½ miles (4km). Open-top bus tours are a popular way to see the city, but if you have the time the most enjoyable way is to explore the city on foot. Beyond the walls, the **National Railway Museum** is the keeper of Britain's railway heritage and is well worth visiting for its huge displays from the golden age of steam.

✚ 41C2

ℹ George Hudson Street
YO1 6WR ☎ 01904
554455;
www.visityork.org

Jorvik Viking Centre

✉ Coppergate

☎ 01904 643211

✋ Moderate

National Railway Museum

✉ Leeman Road

☎ 01904 611112

✋ Moderate

Below: *York Minster – 250 years of skilled craft that houses the finest collection of stained glass in England*

10
Yorkshire Dales

A series of charming upland valleys, each with a distinctive character, makes up this popular National Park.

Below: the Yorkshire Dales has a network of ancient tracks like High Lane in Wensleydale

Lying astride the Pennines in the north of England, the Yorkshire Dales are a popular area of wild and rugged moorlands, rivers, streams (here called becks and valleys (the 'dales'), patterned by hedgerows, drystone walls, farmsteads and villages. The principal dales – Airedale, Wharfedale, Nidderdale, Wensleydale and Swaledale – have a distinctive character and culture and, even until modern times, noticeably different dialects. But the landscape unites them, with its open fells, heather moors, limestone and gritstone crags and close-cropped turf.

The region is honeycombed with cave systems so complex that some remain unexplored. There are show caves at Clapham and near Grassington. Grassington itself, a delightful village around a small square in Wharfedale, has a fine museum of Dales life. Nearby Bolton Priory is a medieval abbey picturesquely sited in meadowland, surrounded by woods and rolling moorland. Airedale's biggest attraction is Malham Cove, a huge 250ft (76m) inland cliff which dominates the head of the valley. Wensleydale, famous for its cheese, lies further north and boasts several spectacular waterfalls as well as the busy little market town of Hawes at its centre. Swaledale is altogether more remote and wild, its northern fringe sloping off into the high moorlands of the North Pennines. Lead mining was very important here until the end of the 19th century and the area's gills (side valleys) bear the romantically healed scars of this former industry.

The surrounding towns such as Settle and Ingleton in the west, Skipton (► 52) in the south and Richmond (► 49) and Leyburn in the east make excellent centres for exploration. This is splendid walking country, spanned by the Pennine Way National Trail and other recreational paths, and a popular challenge walk links the region's three highest peaks: Pen-y-Ghent, Whernside and Ingleborough.

✝ 40B2

✉ Yorkshire Dales National Park Authority, Colvend, Hebden Road, Grassington, Skipton, West Yorkshire BD23 5LB

☎ 01756 752748; www.yorkshiredales. org.uk

? For a free copy of the excellent 'What's On' booklet, published by the Yorkshire Tourist Board, call ☎ 01904 707961

What to See

Above: *Buckingham Palace*
Right: *fun on the beach*

London

London is one of Europe's biggest cities, with a population of over 7 million souls, spreading for more than 620sq miles (992sq km) from its heart along the River Thames. It is a place with unequalled charisma and an almost tangible air of constant excitement that comes as much from the amazingly cosmopolitan make-up of its resident population as from the 'buzz' of a capital city. Yet, in spite of the constant activity, there are many oases of peace and quiet. London's public parks, gardens, museums and historic churches rival the best in the world – many tucked away from the traffic congestion and the brouhaha of everyday life. 'Shopaholics' will be in some kind of heaven here, whether rubbing shoulders with the high and mighty in Harrods or, at the other extreme, bustling with the hoi polloi at one of the many weekend street markets.

'Earth has not anything to show more fair: Dull would he be of soul who could pass by a sight so touching in its majesty'

WILLIAM WORDSWORTH (1770–1850)
Sonnet composed on
Westminster Bridge

———————•———————

BRITISH MUSEUM ✪✪✪

The British Museum, the world's first public museum, was created in 1753, following the death of Sir Hans Sloane, whose collection of over 80,000 artefacts was sold to the British government. The museum, the largest in the UK, moved to its present site in 1823 and contains over 6 million items. Worth singling out are the Elgin Marbles, the Rosetta Stone, the Oriental Collection, the Mexican Gallery and the Lindisfarne Gospels.

🚩 31D4
✉ Great Russell Street, Bloomsbury
☎ 020 7636 1555, 020 7323 8000; www.thebritishmuseum.ac.uk
🕐 Sat–Wed 10–5.30, Thu, Fri 10–8.30. Closed 1 Jan, Good Friday, 24–26 Dec
🍴 Café (£); restaurant (££)
🚇 Holborn, Tottenham Court Road, Russell Square
♿ Excellent
🎟 Free

Left: *the British Museum houses many of Britain's greatest treasures*

BUCKINGHAM PALACE ✪

Built in 1703 as the Duke of Buckingham's city residence, on the site of a brothel, the Palace, which was renovated during the 19th century, has served as the monarch's permanent London home since the time of Victoria. It is open to visitors for two months of the year, but provides a glimpse into only 18 of the 600 rooms; queues at the ticket office opposite in Green Park can be considerable. The Changing of the Guard, which takes place daily at around 11:30, from April to July and on alternate days the rest of the year, doesn't involve queuing, and is the most popular reason for visiting the palace.

🚩 30C2
✉ The Mall
☎ Recorded information 020 7799 2331; credit card bookings 020 7321 2233
🕐 Aug and Sep daily 9:30–4:30
🚇 Green Park, Hyde Park Corner, St James's Park, Victoria
♿ Excellent (wheelchair users must prebook)
🎟 Very expensive

COVENT GARDEN ✪✪✪

Taking its name from a medieval convent garden, the bustling, pedestrianised piazza of Covent Garden was laid out by Inigo Jones in 1631, and was initially a very fashionable address. Forty years later, it had developed into the main London fruit and vegetable market, and became a notorious red light district. In the 1830s the area was cleaned up and the splendid iron and glass hall you see today was built to house the market, which it did until this moved south of the river to Vauxhall in 1974. Today only some arcading and St Paul's Church remain of the original piazza. Buskers and other entertainers are a daily sight. The Royal Opera House (► 112) reopened in 1999 after a major refurbishment.

🚩 31D3
🍴 Numerous (£–££)
🚇 Covent Garden

29

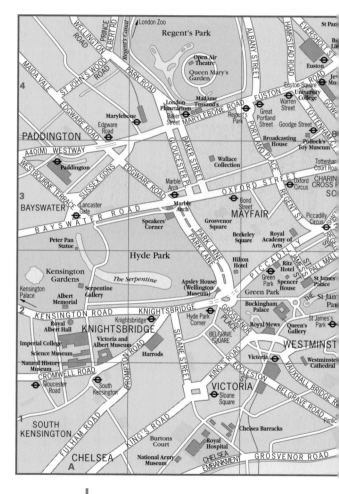

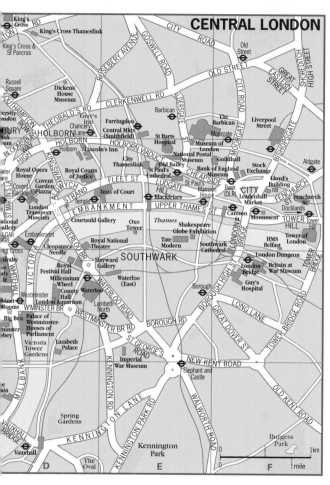

CENTRAL LONDON

King's Cross
King's Cross Thameslink
King's Cross & St Pancras
Russell Square
Dickens House Museum
CLERKENWELL RD
ROSEBERY AVENUE
GOSWELL ROAD
CITY ROAD
OLD STREET
Old Street
CITY ROAD
GREAT EASTERN STREET
SHOREDITCH HIGH STREET
SOUTHAMPTON ROW
'ersity ndon
BURY
BLOOMSBURY
THEOBALD'S RD
Gray's Inn
Chancery Lane
Central Mkt (Smithfield)
Farringdon
Barbican
The Barbican
Liverpool Street
ALDERSGATE ST
HOLBORN
HOLBORN
HIGH
KINGSWAY
Holborn
Lincoln's Inn
HOLBORN VIADUCT
St Barts Hospital
St Pauls Cathedral
Museum of London
National Postal Museum
Guildhall
Moorgate
MOORGATE
BISHOPSGATE
ater are
Royal Opera House
Covent Garden Piazza
Royal Courts of Justice
FLEET ST
City Thameslink
Old Bailey
CHEAPSIDE
Bank of England Museum
Stock Exchange
Aldgate
Covent Garden
ST MARTIN'S LA
ALDWYCH
STRAND
Inns of Court
LUDGATE HILL
St Paul's
Mansion House
Bank (DLR)
CITY
Lloyd's Building
FENCHURCH ST
Fenchurch St
ational allery
LGAR ARE
Temple
Blackfriars
Leadenhall Market
Docklands
g Cross
London Transport Museum
EMBANKMENT
UPPER THAMES ST
Cannon St
Monument
TOWER HILL
Tower Hill
Courtauld Gallery
Oxo Tower
Thames
Shakespeare Globe Exhibition
HMS Belfast
Tower of London
TOWER BRIDGE
irally
eds fe
Embankment
Cleopatra's Needle
Royal National Theatre
Tate Modern
Southwark Cathedral
London Bridge
LONDON BRIDGE
London Dungeon
Britain at War Museum
inet Rooms
Hayward Gallery
SOUTHWARK
Big Ben
inster bey
Westminster
Royal Festival Hall
Millennium Wheel
County Hall
London Aquarium
Waterloo
Waterloo (East)
Lambeth North
Borough
Guy's Hospital
BOROUGH HIGH ST
LONG LANE
GREAT DOVER ST
TOWER BRIDGE ROAD
WHITEHALL
VICTORIA
WATERLOO RD
W'MINSTER BR
WESTMINSTER BR RD
BOROUGH RD
Palace of Westminster - Houses of Parliament
Victoria Tower Gardens
Lambeth Palace
MILLBANK
e ain
Imperial War Museum
ST GEORGE'S ROAD
KENNINGTON RD
Elephant and Castle
NEW KENT ROAD
OLD KENT ROAD
WALWORTH ROAD
VAUXHALL BRIDGE
Vauxhall
Spring Gardens
KENNINGTON LANE
KENNINGTON PARK RD
KENNINGTON ROAD
Kennington Park
Burgess Park
The Oval
D
E
F
0   1km
0   ½ mile

✚ 31F3

Above: *Canary Wharf
Tower in London's
Docklands is Britain's
tallest building*

DOCKLANDS ✪

Containerisation brought the decline of London's
enormous dockland area. For 20 years this part of the city
lay derelict, until the 1980s when a development corpo-
ration was established to provide residential and office
accommodation. The centrepiece is the Canary Wharf
tower, at 800ft (244m) Britain's tallest building, designed
by Cesar Pelli. The area is connected to central London by
the Docklands Light Railway (DLR), with its distinctive
driverless trains.

✚ 80B2

GREENWICH ✪✪✪

Steeped in royal and naval history, Greenwich (pronounced
Gren-itch), boasts some of London's finest architecture in
the Royal Observatory, the Old Royal Naval College,
Queen's House (a miniature
palace built for the wife of James
I) and the National Maritime
Museum. The *Cutty Sark* is
docked here and Greenwich Park
is one of the city's most attractive.
Best approached by boat or on the
Docklands Light Railway.
Greenwich is also the site of the
Greenwich Meridian.

> ### DID YOU KNOW?
>
> The *Cutty Sark*, formerly a tea ship, was named
> from Robert Burn's *Tam O'Shanter*, in which
> Tam is chased by Nannie, a witch wearing a
> short linen dress, or 'cutty sark'. The figurehead
> on the ship shows Nannie clutching the hair
> from the tail of Tam's horse.

✚ 30B2
🍴 The Lido café (£)
Ⓢ Several including Marble
Arch and Hyde Park Corner

Serpentine Gallery
☎ 020 7402 6075
🕐 Daily during exhibitions
Ⓢ Lancaster Gate, South
Kensington
♿ Excellent
🆓 Free

HYDE PARK ✪✪✪

Hyde Park is the largest and most famous of the central
London parks. If you enter at Hyde Park Corner, you pass
through Constitution Arch, commemorating Wellington's
victory at Waterloo. Approach from Oxford Street, and
you'll pass Marble Arch, designed by Nash in 1827 to
imitate the Arch of Constantine in Rome; until 1851 it
stood in front of Buckingham Palace (➤ 29). Near Marble
Arch is Speaker's Corner, a platform for cranks, hecklers
and religious extremists, and an ideal place for a little light
entertainment. The **Serpentine Gallery**, to the west of the
Serpentine lake, contains contemporary art exhibitions.

London: Royal Parks

The Royal Parks are wonderful oases of green in the very heart of London; this walk links four of them.

Begin from Westminster, opposite the Houses of Parliament. Cross Parliament Square and go into Great George Street. Take the first right, and turn into St James's Park.

St James's is the oldest and most attractive of the central London parks, established by Henry VIII in the 1530s.

Keep to the left of the lake until you can cross it by a bridge.

The views from the bridge are splendid in both directions: face the impressive buildings of Whitehall, and behind you lies Buckingham Palace.

Over the bridge, turn left, and go up to join The Mall. Cross this and walk towards Buckingham Palace. Keep right, by the edge of Green Park, and up Constitution Hill. Tackle the Green Park and Hyde Park Corner subways, as if going to Hyde Park station, but continue instead up to the Park.

Hyde Park (►32) originally belonged to the Church, until Henry VIII seized it to use as hunting grounds.

By keeping to the eastern side of the Park you eventually find your way to Marble Arch. Go through the subway complex here, to exit 14. Go forward into Oxford Street until you can turn left into Portman Street. Turn right into Portman Square and when you reach Wigmore Street, go left along another side of Portman Square, and forward into Baker Street. At the far end of Baker Street, continue the short distance to reach Regent's Park, the last of the Royal Parks. Return from Baker Street Station.

Distance
4¼ miles (7km)

Time
3–4 hours including stops

Start point
Houses of Parliament
🚩 31D2

End point
Regent's Park
🚩 30B4

Lunch
Serpentine Cafe (£)

Above: take it easy and enjoy a concert in St James's Park

31D2
Jubilee Gardens, South Bank
0870 500 0600; www.ba-londoneye.com
Waterloo
Excellent   Expensive

31E3
London Wall
020 7600 3699
Millburn Restaurant (£)
Barbican, Moorgate
Excellent
Free

31D3
Trafalgar Square
020 7747 2484, recorded information 020 7747 2885; www.nationalgallery.org.uk
Mon–Sun 10–6, Wed 10–9. Closed 1 Jan, 24–26 Dec
Café (£), Brasserie (££)
Charing Cross
Excellent   Free

London Eye pod

LONDON EYE (BRITISH AIRWAYS)

Take an exhilerating 30-minute ride on the world's largest observation wheel, erected for the millennium. An instantly recognisable addition to London's skyline, on a clear day you can see 25 miles (40km) out over the city. It is essential to book in advance to avoid the long queues.

MUSEUM OF LONDON

Beginning with a Prehistoric Gallery, then progressing chronologically, the Museum of London tells the story of the history of the capital. Very few of London's ancient buildings remain, but since World War II many important Roman, Saxon and Tudor discoveries have been made and are on display here. You will also find the Lord Mayor's Coach, a replica of a Newgate prison cell and the story of the Great Fire of London.

NATIONAL GALLERY

Housing over 2,000 paintings, and taking up the whole of the north side of Trafalgar Square, the National Gallery contains one of the finest and most comprehensive collections of Western art in the world. The collection is divided chronologically, beginning with medieval and early Renaissance work, and includes *The Virgin of the Rocks* by Leonardo da Vinci, *Venus and Mars* by Botticelli, *Doge Leonardo Loredan* by Giovanni Bellini and *The Battle of San Romano* by Uccello. Because of the sheer scale of the place, it's a good idea to call into the Micro Gallery in the Sainsbury Wing, where, with the aid of computers, you can plan your own tour.

Left: *the Natural History Museum is surprisingly entertaining*

NATURAL HISTORY MUSEUM ✪✪

Here the building, constructed in neo-Gothic cathedral style in the 1870s, impresses as much as the exhibits. No visit to the Museum would be complete without seeing the dinosaurs, and (unless you're squeamish about these things) the Creepy Crawlies exhibition – a great favourite with children. This is a far cry from the traditional image of a natural history museum, combining a wealth of content with imaginative new technology.

🕂 30A1
✉ Cromwell Road and Exhibition Road
☎ 020 7942 5000; www.nhm.ac.uk
🕐 Mon–Sat 10–5.50, Sun 11.50
🚇 South Kensington
♿ Excellent
✋ Free

PALACE OF WESTMINSTER ✪✪

Parliament has not always met in London, but the first Palace of Westminster was built here around 1050 by Edward the Confessor, and significantly extended by William the Conqueror. There are two debating chambers, the House of Commons and the House of Lords, and you can queue for a seat in the Visitors' Gallery on 'sitting days', normally weekdays (afternoons only Monday, Tuesday and Thursday) for the Commons and Monday to Thursday afternoons for the Lords, by waiting outside St Stephen's entrance.

🕂 31D2
✉ St Margaret Street (public entrance)
☎ 020 7219 4272; www.parliament.uk (Commons); 020 7219 3107 (Lords)
🚇 Westminster
♿ Few
✋ Free

The best-known feature of the building is the clock tower, Big Ben, though this is more correctly the popular name for its 13.4 ton (13.7 tonne) bell, cast at the Whitechapel Bell Foundry in 1858 and named after Benjamin Hall, First Commissioner of Works at the time. It chimes on the hour, and is the traditional signal throughout Britain that marks the start of a new year.

Left: *the face of Big Ben, the popular time-piece of Britain*

ROYAL BOTANIC GARDENS, KEW ✪✪✪

Containing an outstanding collection of plants, trees and flowers from all parts of the world, Kew Gardens owe their origin to Augusta, the Dowager Princess of Wales and mother of George III. In 1759, she turned part of her estate into a botanical garden, primarily for educational and scientific purposes. By 1841, however, the garden had seriously declined and was handed over to the State. The following year Sir William Hooker was appointed the first official director and the gardens began to acquire their worldwide reputation. They expanded to the present 300 acre (121ha) site at the beginning of the 20th century.

🕂 80A2
✉ Kew, Richmond
☎ 020 8332 5655; www.kew.org
🕐 Telephone for opening times
🍴 The Orangery (£–££), Pavilion Restaurant (£), Kew Bakery (£)
🚇 Kew Gardens
♿ Very good
✋ Moderate

Right: *if you have the energy, the climb to the Whispering Gallery at the top of St Paul's Cathedral is worth the effort*

ST PAUL'S CATHEDRAL ⊕⊕

When Sir Christopher Wren completed St Paul's in 1711 it was hailed as the world's first Protestant cathedral. Work began after the Great Fire of London in 1666 had destroyed the previous cathedral. It continues to dominate the London skyline, towering above many newer buildings. Inside are Flaxman's Nelson Memorial and Steven's Duke of Wellington Monument, as well as the celebrated Whispering Gallery with its eerie acoustic effects. Continue to the Golden Gallery for one of the finest views.

SCIENCE MUSEUM ⊕⊕

One of the world's finest collections of landmarks in industrial history, technological milestones, and truly fascinating objects, the Science Museum gives a wonderful exposition of how things work and how technology has developed. There are 40 galleries; exhibits you wouldn't want to miss include the *Apollo 10* command module, Stephenson's *Rocket*, the prototype computer and the first iron lung. The Museum is renowned for its pioneering interactive hands-on displays (over 2,000) that make any visit a memorable experience.

TATE BRITAIN ⊕⊕

Tate Britain houses the national collection of British art from 1500 to the present, including the highlight, the Turner Bequest, as well as pre-Raphaelite works. Until 2000, the national collections of British and international modern art were housed here, then the international collection went to Bankside, renamed Tate Modern.

TATE MODERN ⊕⊕

Britain's national collection of international modern art from 1900 to the present day. The most influential artists of the 20th century are represented, including Picasso, Matisse, Dalí, Rodin, Gabo and Warhol.

TOWER OF LONDON (▶ 24, TOP TEN)

✚ 31E3
✉ St Paul's Churchyard
☎ 020 7236 4128; recorded information 020 7246 8348
🕐 Mon–Sat 8:30–6; galleries Mon–Sat 9:30–4
🍴 The Crypt Café (£), The Refectory Restaurant (£–££)
🚇 St Paul's
♿ Few 💷 Moderate

✚ 30A2
✉ Exhibition Road, South Kensington
☎ 0870 870 4868
🕐 Daily 10–6
🍴 Museum cafés (£), restaurant (£–££)
🚇 South Kensington
♿ Excellent
💷 Free; charge for some individual attractions

✚ 31D1
✉ Millbank
☎ 020 7887 8000; recorded information 020 7887 8008
🕐 Daily 10–5:50
🚇 Pimlico ♿ Excellent
💷 Free (charge for some exhibitions)

✚ 31E3
✉ Bankside
☎ 020 7887 8008
🕐 Sun–Thu 10–6, Fri, Sat 10–10
🚇 Blackfriars, Southwark
♿ Excellent 💷 Free (charge for some exhibitions)

TRAFALGAR SQUARE ✪✪✪

The heart of London, from where all road distances are measured, Trafalgar Square was designed by John Nash in the 1830s, and built in honour of Lord Nelson following his victory at the Battle of Trafalgar in 1805. The centrepiece is Nelson's Column, 187ft (57m) high, erected between 1839 and 1842.

Close by is the **Church of St Martin-in-the-Fields**, an attractive building, famous for its concerts and its social care unit. There is an art gallery in the crypt, and outside in the grounds is a daily clothes and crafts market.

✚ 31D3
Church of St Martin-in-the-Fields
✉ Trafalgar Square
☎ 020 7839 8362 for concert tickets
🍴 Café-in-the-Crypt (£)
Ⓒ Charing Cross, Leicester Square
♿ Good; no wheelchair access to café
🎟 Free

VICTORIA AND ALBERT MUSEUM (V&A) ✪✪

Originally called the South Kensington Museum, the V&A is dedicated to the applied arts, and was established to house the contents of the Great Exhibition of 1851. Today the museum displays cultural artefacts from around the world, especially from the Orient, and houses one of the world's finest collection of decorative arts. Some 8 miles (13km) and four storeys of corridors and rooms make it essential to obtain a map and index before setting off into the museum.

✚ 30A2
✉ Cromwell Road, South Kensington
☎ 020 7942 2000; www.vam.ac.uk
Ⓒ Daily 10–5.45 (Wed until 10). Closed 24–26 Dec
🍴 Café Espresso (£), The New Restaurant (£–££)
Ⓒ South Kensington
♿ Excellent
🎟 Free
❓ Guided tours

Left: *one of the world's finest collections of decorative art is housed in the ornate splendour of the Victoria and Albert Museum*

WESTMINSTER ABBEY ✪✪✪

Dating from the 13th and 16th centuries, Westminster Abbey stands on the site of a Benedictine monastery which Edward the Confessor (reigned 1042–66) sought to enlarge, close to his Palace of Westminster (► 35). The Abbey has been the setting for the coronation of every British monarch, except Edward V and Edward VIII, since the time of William the Conqueror. Today it is still a church, in use for regular worship, and over 3,000 people, including royalty, are either buried or memorialised here. The best monuments lie beyond the choir-screen, and to see these you have to pay an admission charge.

✚ 31D2
✉ Parliament Square
☎ 020 7222 5897; www.westminster-abbey.org
Ⓒ Mon–Fri 9:30–4:45 and Wed 6–7:45, Sat 9:30–2:45. Closed Sun
🍴 Coffee stands only
Ⓒ Westminster, St James's Park
♿ Good
🎟 Moderate (half price Wed evening)

Northern England

For so long tarred (unjustly) with the dark brush of industrial grime and deprivation, the North of England has done much to clean up its image, where cleaning up was needed. But so many parts of the northern counties have always been arbours of beautiful landscape and rural retreats to rival any in England. The attractions of the Lake District, the Yorkshire Dales, the North York Moors and Northumberland have long been popular and are well known. Perhaps less renowned are the pretty villages and hamlets of Lancashire and Durham and the quiet backwaters of delectable Calderdale. Today bright, bustling and thriving cities – Leeds, Manchester, Liverpool, Sheffield and many more – play a fundamental role in the tourism and leisure industry, enabling visitors to get the best out of their stay in the North.

> *'…it would be out of all doubt more prudent and delightful to be Tees or Wharfe than Rhone.'*
>
> JOHN RUSKIN
> *Praeterita* (1885–9)

Castle Keep is tucked away in the mix of architectural styles in central Newcastle upon Tyne

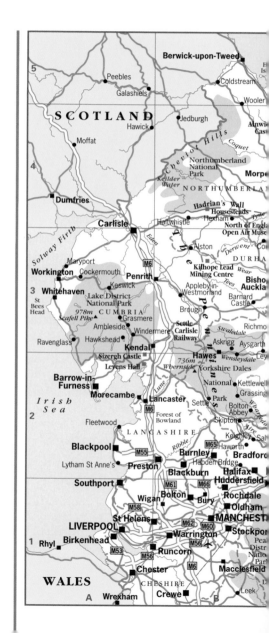

NORTHERN ENGLAND

0   20   40 km

0   10   20   30 miles

wick
Amble

NEWCASTLE UPON TYNE

eamish   Sunderland

Durham

A1(M)

Hartlepool

tockton-
on-Tees   Middlesbrough

Darlington   Whitby

North York Moors
National Park

Scarborough

Thirsk   Helmsley   Pickering

NORTH
YORKSHIRE   Filey

Castle   Flamborough
Ripon   Howard   Head

untains
abbey A1(M)   Bridlington

Knaresborough   Driffield

arrogate   York   EAST RIDING
OF YORKSHIRE

Wharfe   Market
Weighton

LEEDS   HULL

Castleford   Withernsea

WEST   M62
ORKSHIRE   Goole   Humber

ational Coalmining   M18
useum   Scunthorpe   Grimsby

Barnsley Doncaster   M180

SOUTH
ORKSHIRE Kelham Island   Gainsborough   Louth
Museum A1(M)   The Wolds

SHEFFIELD   Worksop   Market
Rasen

M1   NOTTING-   Lincoln
HAMSHIRE   LINCOLNSHIRE

YSHIRE   Mansfield   Newark-
Matlock   on-Trent   Coningsby

C   D

Right: *furnished in Italian Renaissance style, Alnwick Castle, the second largest inhabited castle in England, is home to the Duke of Northumberland*

🔲 40B4
☎ 01665 511100;
www.alnwickcastle.com
🕐 Late Mar–late Oct daily 11–5
🍴 Castle tearoom (£)
♿ Few
💷 Moderate

🔲 40B5
ℹ 106 Marygate TD15 1BN
✉ 01289 330733

Cell Block Museum
✉ Guildhall, Marygate
☎ 01289 330900
🕐 Easter–Sep, Mon–Fri
💷 Cheap

The Royal Border Bridge at Berwick-upon-Tweed, England's most northerly town

ALNWICK CASTLE ✪✪

The 11th-century Alnwick Castle came into the Percy family in 1309, and is the birthplace of Harry Hotspur (1364–1403). Following the revolt against Henry IV and the Battle of Shrewsbury, where Hotspur was killed, the estates were temporarily confiscated. The Duke of Northumberland still lives here, in what is the second largest inhabited castle in England. The magnificent staterooms are furnished in Italian Renaissance style with paintings by Titian, Canaletto and Van Dyck, fine furniture and an exquisite china collection.

BERWICK-UPON-TWEED ✪

England's most northerly town changed hands 14 times during the turbulent period when the English and Scots fought to control the borderlands. The town's 16th-century fortifications form the basis of the massively thick Elizabethan walls encircling the town, which took 11 years to complete. The town has three distinctive bridges: the Royal Border Railway Bridge, built after the style of a Roman aqueduct by Robert Stephenson in the 1840s, contrasts remarkably with the rather modest 15-arch Berwick Bridge, completed in 1624, and the poor, concrete offering of the 1920s' Royal Tweed Bridge. In the centre of town the original jail houses the **Cell Block Museum**, which depicts tales of crime and punishment.

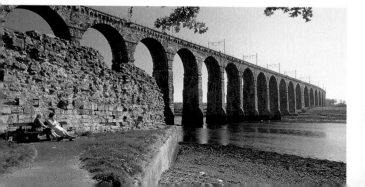

CARLISLE ✪✪

Carlisle is a border city, with a wide pedestrianised market place at its heart. Its name is derived from the Celtic word *caer* meaning fort. Scottish and English names and accents still mingle freely in its covered market and malls, though there is little today to hint at the troubles the city has faced. It was last besieged in 1745 by Bonnie Prince Charlie's Jacobite army. Chief among the city's assets are the castle, the striking red sandstone cathedral, and the **Tullie House Museum & Art Gallery**, which dramatically portrays much of the city's turbulent past, as a Roman frontier settlement and as a border town fought over for centuries. Carlisle is also the terminus for the scenically spectacular Settle–Carlisle railway, providing a regular rail link with West Yorkshire via the delightful countryside of the Eden Valley (► below) and the Yorkshire Dales (► 26, Top Ten).

✚ 40A3
ℹ Old Town Hall ☎ 01228 625600; www.historic-carlisle.org.uk

Tullie House
✉ Castle Street
☎ 01228 534781
🕐 Mon–Sat 10–5, Sun 12–5.
🍴 The Garden Restaurant (£–££)
♿ Excellent
💰 Moderate; half price 10–11

Castle Howard in North Yorkshire is still home to the Howard family

CASTLE HOWARD ✪✪

The splendour of the 18th-century Castle Howard, near Malton, northeast of York, provided the setting for the television adaptation of *Brideshead Revisited*, and is still home to the Howard family. There are richly furnished rooms and an outstanding estate to explore.

✚ 41C2
☎ 01653 648444; www.castlehoward.co.uk
🕐 Mid-Feb–Oct 11–4.45
🍴 Cafe (£–££)
♿ Very good
💰 Expensive

Appleby Castle
✚ 40B3
☎ 01768 351402
🕐 Mar–Nov daily 10–5
🍴 The Castle Tea Shoppe (£)
♿ None
💰 Moderate

EDEN VALLEY ✪✪✪

The River Eden flows down from the Pennine fells through the market towns of Kirkby Stephen and Appleby before heading for the Solway Firth. On either side lie lush green pastures and stone-built communities huddled around village greens. Appleby is a delightful town of sandstone buildings, notably along its main street, with **Appleby Castle** at the top and St Lawrence's Church at the bottom. Each year in June it is the venue for a horse fair, the largest gypsy gathering in England.

Right: *World Heritage Site Fountains Abbey, and the nearby Studley Royal Water Gardens make a popular day out*

✚ 41C2
✉ Studley Park, Fountains, Ripon
☎ 01765 608888; www. fountainabbey.org.uk
🕐 Jan–Mar, Oct–Dec daily 10–4; Apr–Sep 10–6; closed Fri Dec–Jan. Deer park: daily daylight hours. Closed 24–25 Dec
🍴 Restaurant (£–££)
♿ Very good
✋ Moderate

FOUNTAINS ABBEY ✪✪✪

In 1132 thirteen monks, rebelling against the relaxed atmosphere of their parent house, came to Fountains to begin an austere and simple life. When the Dissolution of the Monasteries brought abbey life to an end in the 16th century, they left behind the most complete and largest Cistercian abbey remains in Britain. Too remote to be turned into a country house or plundered for building stone, the abbey remains evoke the spirit of the religious community that lived here for 400 years. Near by, the Studley Royal Water Garden is one of the most spectacular gardens in England and, with the abbey, has been designated a World Heritage Site.

HADRIAN'S WALL (▶ 19, TOP TEN)

✚ 40A3
ℹ Market Cross, Ambleside ☎ 015394 32582

Beatrix Potter Gallery
✉ Main Street, Hawkshead
☎ 01539 436355
🕐 Closed Fri, Sat & Nov–Mar
🍴 Several in village (£–££)
♿ None ✋ Cheap

HAWKSHEAD ✪✪✪

Before the 19th century Hawkshead could not be reached by road, and the narrow streets in the village centre are still inaccessible by car. Wordsworth attended the grammar school, which is now a museum and library. Beatrix Potter's husband, William Heelis, was a local solicitor, and his offices now house the **Beatrix Potter Gallery**, which contains original drawings from her books and tells the story of her life.

✚ 40B2
ℹ 2–4 West Lane ☎ 01535 642329; www. visithaworth.com

Brontë Parsonage Museum
✉ Church Street
☎ 01535 642323
🍴 Cafés in town (£–££)
♿ None
✋ Moderate

HAWORTH ✪✪

On the edge of the Pennine moors, Haworth, scarcely less a literary shrine than Stratford-upon-Avon, is an attractive and busy little town famed for cobbled streets and its association with the Brontë sisters – Charlotte, Emily and Anne, who came to live here in 1820. The Brontës were a close-knit family and their home, now the **Parsonage Museum**, formed the focus of the sisters' world from an early age. The museum displays the Brontë's own furniture and possessions, and is a good starting point for the popular Brontë Trail.

HEBDEN BRIDGE

The town developed in medieval times at a river crossing and crossroads on packhorse trails that fed into the valley, but it was not until mechanisation was introduced in the 18th century that Hebden Bridge began to grow. As its textile industry flourished, the influx of workers meant that houses had to be built up the steep valley sides, giving the town its characteristic 'double-decker' housing. Some of the old mill buildings have been attractively converted into museums, craft galleries and shopping areas. At the heart of the South Pennines, the surrounding landscape of Calderdale, overlooked by the tower on Stoodley Pike, is surprisingly attractive.

> ### DID YOU KNOW?
>
> The high-energy glucose confection, Kendal Mint Cake, was the result of an accident in 1868, when Joseph Wiper was boiling sugar in his sweet shop.

HOLY ISLAND

Formerly known as Lindisfarne, it was on Holy Island that St Aidan of Iona founded a monastery, **Lindisfarne Priory**, in the 7th century, one of the holiest sites of Anglo-Saxon England. This small island, off the east coast, is only accessible by causeway from Beal, and then only when tides permit. St Cuthbert lived and died on the island, which has become a place of pilgrimage. Lindisfarne Castle was built in the 16th century, to defend the harbour from marauding Scots, and its museum includes a collection of inscribed stones, all that remain of the first monastery.

KENDAL

The limestone-grey buildings of this busy market town conceal a maze of yards and 'ginnels'. They are a delight to explore: one contains a row of charming almshouses, still in use. Above the town rise the ruins of Kendal Castle, birthplace of Katherine Parr (1512–48), the last wife of Henry VIII. **Abbott Hall Art Gallery**, near the church, includes work by Ruskin, Constable and Turner. The Museum of Lakeland Life in the adjacent stables contains Arthur Ransome and 'Postman Pat' memorabilia, as well as displays on local history.

Sidebar

✚ 40B2

ℹ New Road ☎ 01422 843831 **◉** Easter–Oct Mon–Fri 9.30–5.30, Sat 10.15–5, Sun 10.30–5; Mon–Fri 10–5, Sat–Sun 10.30–4.15, rest of year

✚ 40B5

Lindisfarne Priory and Museum
☎ 01289 389200
◉ Daily Apr–Sep, 10–6; Oct, 10–5; Nov–Mar, 10–4. Closed 24–26 Dec, 1 Jan
🍴 Café and restaurant in village (£)
♿ Few
♨ Moderate

✚ 40A3

ℹ Town Hall, Highgate ☎ 01539 725758; www.kendaltown.org **◉** Mon–Sat 9–5, Sun 10–4

Abbott Hall Art Gallery
☎ 01539 722464
◉ Apr–Oct, daily 10:30–5; Nov–Mar, daily 10:30–4. Closed Sun & 25 Dec–early Feb
🍴 The Coffee Shop (£)
♿ Few
♨ Moderate
↔ Levens Hall and Topiary Gardens (➤ 47), Sizergh Castle (➤ 52)

The Rochdale Canal in Hebden Bridge. One of the earliest trans-Pennine waterways, it was opened in 1804 and is now used for recreation

40B3

✉ Cowshill, Co Durham

☎ 01388 537505

🕙 Apr–Oct, daily 10:30–5; Nov, Sun only 10:30–4

🍴 Café (£)

♿ Few

💷 Moderate, additional charge for mine visit

KILLHOPE LEAD MINING CENTRE

Bleakly situated at the head of Weardale in the North Pennines, the Killhope Lead Mining Centre is a fascinating legacy from a heavily industrial era, created from one of the largest lead and iron ore mining sites in England. Industrial artefacts and debris lie scattered across an open-air site, including a restored 34ft-high (10m) waterwheel, originally built to power the crushing mills, but the highlight is the chance to go inside one of the mines.

LAKE DISTRICT (➤ 20–21, TOP TEN)

40A2

ℹ 29 Castle Hill ☎ 01524 32878

Lancaster Castle

✉ The Shire Hall

☎ 01524 64998; www.lancastercastle.com

🕙 Mid-Mar to mid-Dec

🍴 Folly Café, Castle Hill (£)

♿ None

💷 Cheap

LANCASTER

Once an important port for the slave trade, much of Lancaster's character comes from the Georgian buildings of this unhappy period, though there was much traffic in mahogany, tobacco, rum and sugar, too. Lancaster Castle, built around 1200 and strengthened in the 15th century, dominates the city and is still used as a crown court and prison, but some sections are open to the public, including the cells where the Pendle Witches were imprisoned. The shopping centre contains many historic buildings, including the Judges Lodging, now a museum, featuring the finely crafted furniture of the local family, the Gillows.

41C2

ℹ The Arcade, City Railway Station ☎ 0113 242 5242; www.leeds.gov.uk 🕙 Daily 9:30–6 (Sat, Sun 10–4 in winter)

Below: the Corn Exchange in Leeds now houses an interesting mix of alternative shops

LEEDS

The largest urban development in Yorkshire and its economic capital, Leeds owes its growth, notably during the 19th century, to wool and to its position as a port on the Leeds–Liverpool and Aire and Calder canals. The area around the canals, which run through the city centre, has been developed to provide a lively waterfront culture of pavement cafés and specialist shops along the water's edge. Following large-scale urban rejuvenation, Leeds has become an outstanding nightlife destination and a major cultural centre, home to Opera North. Leeds' shopping is also a major draw; try the fashionable department store Harvey Nichols for window shopping.

LEVENS HALL AND TOPIARY GARDENS

This magnificent Elizabethan mansion is built around a 13th-century pele tower, and is the family home of the Bagots. On display is a collection of Jacobean furniture, paintings and early English patchwork. The award-winning topiary gardens were laid out in 1694, and feature yews trimmed to the shape of pyramids, peacocks and hats.

40A2
☎ 01539 560321
🕐 House and gardens
Sun–Thu
🍴 Tea Room (£–££)
♿ Few
💷 Moderate
↔ Sizergh Castle (► 52)

LIVERPOOL

The city that produced the Beatles (► 14) is also renowned for its acerbic wit, a remarkable community spirit and fiercely proud loyalty to one of its two major football teams. Liverpool rose to prominence through trade with the Americas, importing sugar, spices, tobacco and slaves. Its historic waterfront is now an important visitor attraction, centred on Albert Dock, where the warehouses comprise probably the greatest grouping of Grade I Listed buildings in the country. They have been converted into a complex of shops, television studios, bars, restaurants and the Tate Gallery Liverpool, which houses an impressive collection of contemporary art. It is complemented by the **Walker Art Gallery**, with its collection of European Old Masters, pre-Raphaelite and modern British works.

40A1
ℹ Atlantic Pavilion, Albert Dock ☎ 0906 680 6886; www.visitliverpool.com
🕐 Daily 9–5:30

Walker Art Gallery
✉ William Brown Street
☎ 0151 478 4199
🕐 Mon–Sat 10–5, Sun 12–5. Closed 1 Jan, 23–26 Dec
🍴 The Walker Coffee Shop (£)
♿ Excellent
💷 Moderate

Manchester was the first English city to reintroduce trams to ease city centre traffic congestion

MANCHESTER

Once the world's major cotton-milling centre, Manchester, with its spruced-up Victorian buildings, extensive shopping, plentiful restaurants and enviable nightlife, is arguably one of the trendiest places in England. Manchester has undergone an urban makeover unequalled in Britain, boosted by the phenomenal success of Manchester United football team, both on the field and on the stock market. The area known as Castlefield, site of a Roman fort, is today the focus of Manchester's tourism industry. Many of the surrounding Victorian warehouses have been converted into apartments, hotels and tourist attractions. **Urbis** is a new kind of museum in a dramatic glass building with interactive exhibits that lead you on a journey through life in cities around the world.

40B1
ℹ Town Hall Extension, Lloyd Street ☎ 0161 234 3157; www.destination manchester.com

Urbis
✉ Cathedral Gardens
☎ 0161 907 9099, information line 0161 605 8200; www.urbis.org.uk
🕐 Daily 10–6
🍴 Conservatory Café (£–££)
♿ Very good
💷 Moderate

41C1

Caphouse Colliery, New Road, Overton, Wakefield

01924 848806

Daily 10–5

Excellent Moderate

41C4

128 Grainger Street
0191 277 8000; www.newcastle.tourism.com

Laing Gallery

New Bridge Street

0191 232 7734

Mon–Sat 10–4:50, Sun 2–4:50

The Café Laing (£–££)

Excellent

Free

40B3

Beamish, Co Durham

01207 234184; www.beamish.org.uk

Apr–Oct, daily 10–5; Nov–Mar 10–4

Tearoom on site (£–££)

Few

Expensive

NATIONAL COAL MINING MUSEUM

This award-winning museum offers guided tours underground in original workings to see methods and conditions of mining from the early 1800s. There are extensive indoor and outdoor displays, a working steam winder, a train ride and pit ponies.

NEWCASTLE UPON TYNE

Capital of northeast England, Newcastle has survived the decline in many of its traditional industries, like ship building and coal mining. The oldest part of the city is Quayside, now a fashionable oasis with restaurants, pubs, book and antique shops and a Sunday market. The 'new castle' dates from the time of William I ('the Conqueror', reigned 1066–87), though the city's economic wealth grew from a regional monopoly on coal exportation introduced in Elizabethan times. The city has a number of fine galleries and theatres, in particular the **Laing Gallery**, which focuses on 19th-century art.

NORTH OF ENGLAND OPEN AIR MUSEUM, BEAMISH

Buildings from all over the region have been reassembled at Beamish. Many of the costumed guides have real-life experiences and are delighted to chat about their past times. The museum vividly illustrates life in the northeast of England in the early 1800s and 1900s, and includes a colliery village, railway station and goods yard, a 19th-century manor, and a north country town.

RICHMOND ⚫⚫

The town is a gem, an open-air museum of the grandest kind, dominated by its outstanding castle, built by the first Earl of Richmond, Alan Rufus. Centred on a huge cobbled market square with radiating wynds (narrow alleys), the town contains numerous Georgian buildings, but its most unusual building is the defunct Holy Trinity Church, which houses the Green Howards regimental museum.

SALTAIRE ⚫⚫⚫

Built between 1852 and 1872 by Sir Titus Salt, the village, on the River Aire, is a perfectly preserved vision of his industrial Utopia, modelled on buildings of the Italian Renaissance. It was originally constructed in open countryside, to provide Salt's mill workers with the benefits of fresh air, though it is now surrounded by urban sprawl. The mill, which is larger than St Paul's Cathedral in London, was once the biggest factory in the world, and was the centre of a small conglomeration of schools, hospitals, houses, parks, baths and wash-houses. The **1853 Gallery** displays the world's largest collection of the works of Bradford-born artist, David Hockney.

SHEFFIELD ⚫⚫

Until 1997, Sheffield was as far from a tourist destination as you could imagine. Then came the smash hit film *The Full Monty*, a tale of unemployed steelworkers turned male strippers, and suddenly Sheffield was the *in* place. Destination Sheffield organises Full Monty Tours of places connected with the film; contact the TIC for information.

The **Kelham Island Museum**, a mile or so north of the centre, tells the story of Sheffield, its industry and life, and houses the largest working steam engine in Britain. Reconstructed workshops, working cutlers and craftspeople demonstrate the traditional 'Made in Sheffield' skills, and there's a 'hands-on' experience for children to discover how steel is made, as well as interactive exhibits about energy, its uses and conservation. Getting around Sheffield is easy if you use the new Supertram service, which rumbles around the city centre.

✚ 40B3
ℹ️ Friary Gardens, Victoria Road ☎ 01748 850252; www.richmond.org.uk
🕐 Easter–Oct, daily 9:30–5:30; Nov–Mar, Mon–Sat 9:30–4:30
🍽 Numerous in town (£–£££)

✚ 40B2
ℹ️ 2 Victoria Road ☎ 01274 774993 🕐 Daily 10–6

1853 Gallery
✉️ Salts Mill, Victoria Road
☎ 01274 531163
🕐 Daily 10–6. Closed 25–26 Dec
🍽 Diner, fish restaurant (£–££),
♿ Very good
✋ Free

✚ 41C1
ℹ️ 1 Tudor Square ☎ 0114 201 1011; www.sheffieldcity.co.uk

Kelham Island Museum
✉️ Alma Street, Sheffield
☎ 0114 272 2106
🕐 Mon–Thu 10–4, Sun 11–4:45 (closed Fri–Sat)
🍽 Café (£)
♿ Very good
✋ Moderate

Above: *Richmond Castle*
Left: *Newcastle's Tyne Bridge has become a symbol of the city*

49

Food & Drink

It is virtually impossible to identify an English cuisine in the way that you might a French style – yet if such a thing exists, it is probably associated with good, plain cooking of fresh ingredients. In the mid-20th century it became characterised as 'meat and two veg' or 'school dinners', a sometimes affectionate reflection on the fare served up in school canteens.

Above: Bakewell puddings (not tarts) are a popular and sticky delight

For many, 'English' means hearty meat pies, soggy vegetables and heavy desserts such as bread-and-butter-pudding, inevitably served with custard. In recent years 'nouvelle English' has taken a lighter look at the old favourites, and you'll find new takes on traditional menus in pubs and restaurants across the country. And don't forget the sandwich was an English invention.

Cheese

Cheeses are perhaps the most readily identifiable regional specialities. Cheddar (originally from Somerset) is the dominant style, but avoid the plastic supermarket variety and seek out the traditionally made from somewhere like Chewton Dairy in the Mendip Hills (☎ 01761 241666). Cheshire, Lancashire and Wensleydale are crumbly white cheeses, the prefix 'tasty' often used to describe sharper, more mature varieties. They go very well with fruitcake. Central England produces the orangey coloured Red Leicester, the smooth and herby Sage Derby and, most famously, the mature, blue-veined Stilton (delicious with a crisp apple). You'll find the best ranges of cheese are available at specialist delicatessens and farm stalls in traditional markets.

Right: try the traditional full English breakfast

Meat and Fish

When it comes to meat, England is usually associated with beef, whether grilled as steak, roasted as a joint and served with Yorkshire pudding (savoury batter), or cooked slowly with root vegetables in a stew. Look out for local specialities of sausages; Cumberland are long and spicy, Lincolnshire, mild and herb flavoured. Black pudding, made with offal, is popular in the northern counties. Lamb too, is a popular ingredient but vegetarian food is also well established.

As you might expect, seafood is important. On the east coast, Craster is famous for its smoked kippers and Whitby for its crabs. In the southeast, whelks, jellied eels, cockles and mussels are all popular. Wherever you are in England, you're never far from a fish and chip shop, selling cod or haddock fried in batter and served with chips. They're best eaten straight from the wrapper, and sprinkled with salt and vinegar.

Cakes and Ale

Tea time may no longer be *the* afternoon event, but the English retain a fondness for cakes. A Lancashire Eccles cake is sweet mincemeat wrapped in pastry; gingerbread in Grasmere, Cumbria is a delicious, thin, crumbly affair more like a biscuit; and Derbyshire's Bakewell Pudding is commonly recognised as a jam tart topped with sponge.

There are English wines, though the climate means only the whites are generally up to world standards. In beers, you will find the global lager brands available alongside the peculiarly English ales. Served in pint glasses, the best of these are the so-called real ales, which continue to mature in their barrels after leaving the brewery. The dominant varieties are the bitters, such as Tetleys or Courage Best, the darker and usually less strong milds (Banks's is very popular in central England), and the pale ales, of which there is a wide range of locally produced varieties. In western England, traditional cider is still the favourite drink in pubs for many locals.

Above: champagne in Sweetings, London's oldest seafood restaurant Below: many traditional English beers glory in their strange and intriguing names

+ 40A2
☎ 015395 60070
⊙ Easter–Oct Mon–Thu,
  Sun 1.30–5.30; gardens
  12:30–5:30
🍴 Castle Tea Room (£)
♿ Few
✋ Moderate

+ 40B2
ℹ 35 Coach Street
  ☎ 01756 792809;
  www.skiptononline.co.uk
  ⊙ Mon–Sat 10–5 (10–4
  in winter)

Skipton Castle
☎ 01756 792442
🍴 Tea room (£)
♿ None
✋ Moderate

+ 41C3
ℹ Langbourne Road
  ☎ 01947 602674

Captain Cook Memorial Museum
✉ Grape Lane
☎ 01947 601900
🍴 Plenty near by
♿ None
✋ Moderate

SIZERGH CASTLE

The ancestral home of the Strickland family for over 760 years, Sizergh Castle, near Kendal, is built around a 14th-century pele tower, which was extended in Elizabethan times. The castle is surrounded by attractive gardens and contains some fine examples of oak furniture and carved wooden chimney-pieces.

SKIPTON ⊗⊗

At the southern edge of the Yorkshire Dales National Park (► 26), the market town of Skipton is commonly known as the 'gateway to the Dales', and traces its history back to the 7th century when it was known as Sceptone, or 'Sheeptown'. It is dominated by **Skipton Castle** at the top of the main street, reconstructed in the 14th century and remodelled by the redoubtable Lady Anne Clifford in the 17th. Canal trips are available on the Leeds–Liverpool Canal which passes through the town which is a fine base for the exploration of the southern dales.

WHITBY ⊗⊗⊗

The Captain Cook associations, the atmospheric ruins of its 13th-century abbey, its fishing harbour and quiet charm combine to make Whitby an agreeable and fascinating place to visit and one of Yorkshire's most popular resorts. All Cook's ships were built here, and the home of John Walker, to whom Cook was apprenticed, has been converted into a **museum**. The town is bolstered by steep cliffs and divided by the River Esk. The Abbey stands by St Mary's Church on the clifftop above the east side of the town. The church is reached by the 199 steps of the Church Stairs, which featured in Bram Stoker's *Dracula* and a Dracula Trail can be followed across the town.

YORK (► 25, TOP TEN)

YORKSHIRE DALES (► 26, TOP TEN)

Above: *Whitby's houses seem to grow straight from its fishing harbour*

Central England

The 'Heart of England' is easy to reach and explore. Throughout the region, which extends from Derbyshire in the north to Worcestershire and Warwickshire in the south, you'll find a wealth of historic houses, castles and stately homes, whose design and antique treasures are rivalled only by the splendour of the grounds within which they are set. You'll find outstanding opportunities to take part in, or watch, sport, to enjoy a wide-ranging cuisine and to explore the bustling regional cities such as Derby, Nottingham, Leicester, Birmingham and Coventry. Central England is relatively unfrequented by visitors, so it's perhaps here that you have the greatest opportunity of finding a taste of real England...probably tea-flavoured!

> *'There was a rocky valley between Buxton and Bakewell...divine as the vale of Tempe; you might have seen the gods there morning and evening – Apollo and the sweet Muses of the light.'*

JOHN RUSKIN
(1819–1900)

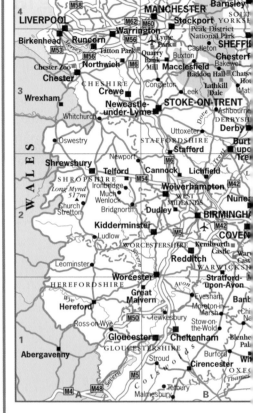

Below: *Gas Street Basin, Birmingham, is part of a spectacular waterfront development built around the old canal network*

✚ 54B2

ℹ 130 Colmore Row, Victoria Square ☎ 0121 202 5099; www. beinbirmingham.com
🕐 Daily 9.15–5.30

BIRMINGHAM ●●

Birmingham's reputation is grim, but once you escape New Street station, Digbeth bus station or the chaotic ring roads, you'll find a city full of vitality, especially in the award-winning waterfront development in Brindley Place, built around the old canal network. The 'city of 1001 trades' was the proving ground for the founders of the Industrial Revolution – steam pioneers James Watt and Matthew Bolton, the inventor of gas lighting William Murdock, and chemist John Priestley. Now again facing a huge city centre transformation, Birmingham's story can be found in the city's excellent museums and galleries, among which the state-of-the-art National Sea Life Centre and the Birmingham Museum and Art Gallery in Chamberlain Square are worth singling out. The latter has a fine collection of pre-Raphaelite paintings.

CENTRAL ENGLAND

Blenheim Palace contains a number of rooms dedicated to the wartime prime minister, Sir Winston Churchill

England's second city, Birmingham today is a major jewellery manufacturing centre, and the Jewellery Quarter a good place to explore. You can walk there from the city centre in about quarter of an hour, or take a train from Moor Street. Look out for the *Jewellery Quarter Magazine*, which includes a walk around the centre that passes the Chamberlain Clock and other interesting sights.

National Sea Life Centre
Brindley Place
0121 633 4700
Moderate

Museum and Art Gallery
Chamberlain Square
0121 303 2834
Free

BLENHEIM PALACE ✪✪

The imposing 18th-century palace of Blenheim is the family seat of the Duke of Marlborough and was designed by Sir John Vanbrugh. It contains several rooms dedicated to Sir Winston Churchill, the wartime prime minister, who was born here and is buried in the church at Bladon, not far away. The nearby village of Woodstock has royal associations dating from Saxon times when the area was used as a hunting ground.

54B1
Woodstock, Oxfordshire
01993 811325; www. blenheimpalace.com
Mid-Mar to Oct, daily 10:30–5:30; park all year, daily 9–5
Restaurant (££)
Good Expensive

55

Lathkill Dale

Distance
6 miles (10km)

Time
3–4 hours including stops

Start point
Bakewell
➕ 54B3

End point
Youlgreave
➕ 54B3

Lunch
The Farmyard pub, Youlgreave
(£–££)

Visiting one of the most delightful of the Derbyshire dales, this walk is linear, so check the times of the buses back to Bakewell from Youlgreave before you set out.

Walk up King Street and turn into South Church Street and then left into Yeld Road. After 100yds (91m), turn right onto a flight of stone steps, and at the top go up a driveway and then an alleyway. At the far end, go past houses and alongside a playing field. Cross a road and go along the right-hand edge of school grounds, then, after two fields, turn left alongside a wall to reach a valley bottom. Turn right, and soon bear left onto a lane for Over Haddon. Go through Over Haddon, turning left at the end down to meet the River Lathkill. Turn right and walk up the valley for 2 miles (3.2km).

The first part of the dale is wooded, giving way to open, rocky scenery that typifies the contrasts of these dales.

As the dale narrows, cross a footbridge on the left and enter Cales Dale. After about 300yds (273m), cross the dale to climb steps on the other side, entering a sloping field. A well-marked route leads up to Calling Low Farm and across fields to a road. Turn left and immediately branch right, then right again behind a car park. Follow a lane down fields to a road below, and there turn left to follow the road into Youlgreave.

Above: *Lathkill is indisputably one of Derbyshire's loveliest dales*

Take a little time to explore this lovely village before returning to Bakewell by bus (No. 171). The bus stop is on the main street in Youlgreave.

Left: *the cliff railway in Bridgnorth links High and Low towns*

BRIDGNORTH ✪✪✪

Bridgnorth, on the River Severn, was once an important port. The old walled town (High Town) is built on a sandstone cliff, and linked to the Low Town by the oldest and steepest inland funicular in England. Check out the old town hall, which has some stunning stained glass.

The town's station is now the northern terminus of the Severn Valley Railway, Britain's longest restored standard-gauge line which runs steam trains to Kidderminster.

🕂 54A2
🛈 Listley Street (in library)
☎ 01746 763257 ◍
Mon–Sat 10–5, Sun (in winter) 11–4

BUXTON ✪✪

There's a relaxing and genteel air about Buxton (named Aquae Arnemetiae by the Romans), one of the highest market towns in England. It even has its own natural spring, the source of its 18th-century popularity, which you can see in the Natural Mineral Baths. Opposite, you can help yourself to mineral water from St Anne's Well, next to the Pump Room, which houses an art gallery. Although the 5th Duke of Devonshire's grand design to make Buxton rival Bath and Cheltenham as a spa resort never quite made it, the plan did see the construction of some distinguished buildings, of which The Crescent, modelled on the Royal Crescent in Bath, is a fine example. **Poole's Cavern**, to the southwest, is worth exploring for its stalactites and stalagmites, and a short walk from there to Solomon's Temple, a 19th-century folly, provides a fine view over the town.

🕂 54B3
🛈 The Crescent ☎ 01298 25106;
www.visitbuxton.co.uk
◍ Daily Mar–Oct, 9:30–5; Nov–Feb, 10–4

Poole's Cavern
✉ Buxton Country Park
☎ 01298 26978;
www.poolescavern.co.uk
◍ Mar–Oct, daily, 10–5
🍴 Shop selling coffees and teas
▥ Moderate
♿ Few

CASTLETON ✪✪

Dominated by the imposing ruins of Peveril Castle, the neat village of Castleton is popular both with walkers, who come to enjoy this particularly scenic part of the Peak District (► 13) and visitors who come to explore the subterranean world of its caverns – The Peak, Treak Cliff, Speedwell and Blue John. **Peveril Castle**, from which the town gets its name, sits high above Cave Dale and gazes across the valley to another stronghold, an Iron-Age fort on the imposing, but crumbling, Mam Tor.

🕂 54B3
🛈 Castle Street ☎ 01433 620679

Peveril Castle
✉ Market Place
☎ 01433 620613
▥ Cheap
♿ None

57

CHATSWORTH HOUSE ✪✪✪

The home of the Dukes of Devonshire for over 400 years, Chatsworth is among the finest houses in England, and contains one of the richest collections of fine and decorative art in private hands, including works by Tintoretto and Rembrandt. The massive formal gardens are tiny in comparison to the enormous park, designed by Capability Brown, which surrounds the house. There is an adventure playground in the park and a farm shop selling produce from the estate.

54B3
✉ Bakewell
☎ 01246 582204
🕐 Late Mar–mid-Dec, daily 11–5:30
🍴 Carriage House Restaurant (£–££), and cafés
♿ None
💷 Expensive

CHESTER ✪✪

Encircled by medieval and Roman walls (around which there is an informative tour), the heart of Chester is the cluster of Tudor and Victorian buildings that includes the raised arcades of The Rows. This is very much a county town, and an ideal base from which to explore. The Romans built their largest fortress in Britain here, but it was much later, as trade routes with Ireland opened up, that the prosperity of the town grew. The cathedral, built between 1250 and 1540, suffers from Victorian meddling, but remains a commanding feature, worth visiting. Beyond the city

walls you can cruise on the River Dee, or hire rowing boats, while further afield, **Chester Zoo**, on the A41, 3 miles (5km) north of the city, is England's largest.

54A3
ℹ Town Hall, Northgate Street ☎ 01244 402111; www.chestertourism.com
🕐 May–Oct, Mon–Sat 9–7:30, Sun 10–4; Nov–Apr, Mon–Sat, 9–5:30 Sun, 10–4

Chester Zoo
☎ 01244 380280; www.chesterzoo.org
🕐 Daily from 10, but closing variable throughout year
🍴 Oasis Café and Oakfield Restaurant (£–££)
♿ Excellent
💷 Expensive

Right: the Rows in Chester, part of the city's heritage of Tudor and Victorian buildings

COTSWOLDS (▶ 17, TOP TEN)

HADDON HALL ✪✪

Home of the Duke of Rutland, Haddon Hall is a delightful Tudor manor house with Norman and Saxon origins, and has served as the setting for many film and television productions. During the 18th and 19th centuries the hall was virtually abandoned and fell into neglect, which proved to be a saving grace, for it evaded the attentions of the Georgian and Victorian 'improvers'. Most of what you see today dates from the 14th and 15th centuries.

54B3
✉ Bakewell, Derbyshire
☎ 01629 812855; www.haddonhall.co.uk
🕐 Apr–Sep, daily 10:30–5; Oct, Sun–Thu 10:30–4:30
🍴 Restaurant (£–££)
♿ None
💷 Expensive

HEREFORD ✪✪✪

Hereford lies amid beautiful countryside and has been a cathedral city since the 8th century. Indeed it is the Norman **cathedral** which is the real draw. It has the world's largest chained library (with books and manuscripts from the 8th to the 15th century), and the extraordinary Mappa Mundi, a parchment map from 1289, depicting the world radiating from Jerusalem.

54A1

Cathedral
☎ 01432 374200
🍴 Cloisters Café
♿ Very good
💷 Cathedral free; exhibition moderate

IRONBRIDGE GORGE   ✪✪✪

Ironbridge Gorge, the crucible of the Industrial Revolution, is Britain's best centre for industrial archaeology, and today enjoys World Heritage Site status. Centred around the eponymous iron bridge, ten **museums**, which it can take a couple of days to explore, illuminate Abraham Darby's pioneering iron work and life in an industrial region. Best among these are the Museum of the Gorge, the Coalbrookdale Museum of Iron, where it all started, the Coalport China Museum, and the Jackfield Tile Museum, which houses a unique display of Victorian tiles. A 'Passport ticket' is available which allows you to visit all the sites economically.

➕ 54A2
ℹ Ironbridge ☎ 01952 433522, 0800 590258; www.ironbridge.org.uk
🕐 Daily 10–5

Ironbridge Gorge Museums
☎ 01952 432166/433522
🕐 Daily 10–5. Some museums closed Nov–Mar, all closed 1 Jan, 24–25 Dec
💷 Moderate–expensive

KENILWORTH CASTLE   ✪✪

Immortalised by Sir Walter Scott, Kenilworth, and the castle from which he took his inspiration, is predominantly a dormitory of Coventry, but the castle is remarkable.

Begun in the 12th century, it eventually fell into the hands of John of Gaunt, who turned it into a magnificent fortified home. His son, Henry IV, used it as a royal residence, and so it remained until Elizabeth I gave it to Robert Dudley. These red sandstone ruins today are still extensive and imposing.

➕ 54B2
☎ 01926 852078
🕐 Apr–Sep, daily 10–6; Oct 10–5; Nov–Mar 10–4
🍴 Tearoom, Leicester's Barn (£)
♿ Good
💷 Moderate

LICHFIELD   ✪✪

The medieval market town of Lichfield, birthplace of the 17th-century writer Dr Samuel Johnson, is dominated by its distinctive three-spired cathedral tracing its history back over 1,000 years. The town centre has a grid of medieval streets overlaid with later, mostly 18th-century, development and makes for fascinating exploration. Worth seeking out are the Samuel Johnson Museum on Market Square, and the museum commemorating Erasmus Darwin (grandfather of Charles, ▶ 14) on Beacon Street.

➕ 54B2
ℹ Donegal House, Bore Street ☎ 01543 308216; www. lichfield-tourist. co.uk 🕐 Mon–Fri 9–4:45, Sat 9–4:30 (until 2 in winter)

Above: *the original iron bridge at Ironbridge*

59

55C3
9 Castle Hill
☎ 01522 873213;
www.lincolnshiretourism.com
Mon–Thu 9.30–5.30, Fri 9.30–5, Sat–Sun 10–5

LINCOLN

The magnificent triple-towered cathedral of Lincoln dominates the landscape from every approach; it is the third largest church in Britain. The site, on a rocky hill rising from the River Witham on the northwest edge of the Fens, was first occupied by Celts, and was such an important, strategic position that the Romans built one of their four regional capitals of Britain here. Lincoln Castle was built over the original Roman town and uses some of the Roman walls. The Jew's House on Steep Hill is one of the best examples of 12th-century domestic architecture, as well as home to the city's top restaurant.

54A2
Castle Street
☎ 01584 875053;
www.ludlow.org.uk
Mon–Sat 10–5, plus summer Sun 10:30–5

Stokesay Castle
⊠ South of Craven Arms off A49
☎ 01588 672544
♿ Good
🎟 Moderate

LUDLOW

One of England's best-preserved medieval and Georgian towns, Ludlow is a place of endless fascination – surely there is no more impressive pub than The Feathers. The town's Norman castle stands in a commanding position on a hill almost surrounded by rivers. The church, St Laurence's, contains some magnificent misericords, and is a testament to the former wool-trading prosperity of the town. Timber-framed houses and fine Georgian buildings line all the streets, and make this a delightful place to wander. Castle lovers will be unable to resist the short journey northwards to visit **Stokesay**, the finest and best-preserved 13th-century fortified manor house in England.

54B3
⊠ Disley, Stockport
☎ 01663 762023
Apr–Oct, Fri–Tue 1–5
🍴 Tearoom (£)
♿ Good
🎟 Moderate

LYME PARK

Set in a vast woodland deer park with ornamental gardens, Lyme Hall has been transformed from a Tudor house into an excellent Italianate palace and one of the finest houses in Cheshire by the Venetian architect, Leoni. The state rooms are decorated by tapestries, wood carvings and an important collection of English clocks.

Right: *ornate timberwork at the Feathers Hotel in Ludlow*

MALVERN ☺☺

Malvern is a generic name for a delightful string of towns along the base of the Malvern Hills, themselves famed for their water. The main centre is Great Malvern, dominated by its striking priory which has some splendid stained glass. The nearby Malvern Hills are immensely popular walking country and give outstanding views across the surrounding countryside. This was the landscape that inspired Edward Elgar (1857–1934), perhaps the greatest of British composers, who was born not far away, near Worcester, and is buried at Little Malvern.

☩ 54B1
🛈 21 Church Street
☎ 01684 892289;
www.malvernhills.gov.uk
🕐 Daily 10–5 (Sun in winter 10–4)

MUCH WENLOCK ☺☺

The Tudor, Jacobean and Georgian architecture in this quiet, unpretentious little town is perfectly reflected in the magnificent Guildhall, perched solidly on the ancient oak columns of the Butter Market. On the edge of town are the ruins of **Wenlock Priory**, an early 13th-century church and Norman chapter house.

☩ 54A2

Wenlock Priory
☎ 01952 727466
🍴 In Much Wenlock
👋 Cheap

NOTTINGHAM ☺☺

Built on sandstone hills at a crossing point of the River Trent, Nottingham is renowned for its association with the 13th-century freebooter, Robin Hood (Sherwood Forest ► 62). This is one of England's biggest cities, and, in spite of first impressions, a lively, buzzing place, with a good, if changeable, nightlife, and an excellent range of modern shopping facilities. The site of the castle, demolished after the Civil War, and the old lace market are the most interesting places, along with the man-made caves, dating from medieval times, which are most easily accessible through the Broad Marsh shopping centre. Spare time for the Brewhouse Yard Museum on Castle Boulevard, which re-creates 19th-century everyday life and traditional shops. There are many claimants to be the oldest pub in Britain, but Ye Olde Trip to Jerusalem, hacked from the walls below the castle, has a stronger claim than most, and was in use at the time of the 13th-century Crusades. D H Lawrence fans will find his birthplace museum in Eastwood, worth the 10-mile (16.2km) trip to see it.

☩ 55C3
🛈 1–4 Smithy Row ☎ 0115 915 5330; www.
discovernottingham.com
🕐 Mon–Fri 9–5:30, Sat 9–5 (also Sun 10–4 Jul–Aug)

OXFORD (► 22, TOP TEN)

✚ 54B3
✉ Styal, Wilmslow
☎ 01625 527468; www.
quarrybankmill.org.uk
🍴 Mill Kitchen restaurant
Mill Pantry (£)
♿ Good
👣 Moderate

QUARRY BANK MILL, STYAL ⊕⊕

This is a working Georgian cotton mill, built in 1784 by Samuel Greg, and it provides a wonderful insight into the early years of the Industrial Revolution. The group of buildings developed around a 50-ton waterwheel, and charts the growth of cotton textile manufacture. The mill is within the Styal Country Park, along an unspoilt stretch of the River Bollin.

✚ 55C3
Sherwood Forest Country Park Visitor Centre
✉ Edwinstowe
☎ 01623 823202

Clumber Park
☎ 01909 476592
🍴 Restaurant (£–££)
♿ Good
👣 Pedestrians free; cars moderate

SHERWOOD FOREST ⊕

Little remains of Robin Hood's Sherwood Forest except the 450 acres (182ha) of the present country park. Extensive clearance during the 18th century makes it virtually impossible to imagine how this meagre swathe of woodland might ever have concealed a band of outlaws.

Just a few minutes from the visitor centre is the Major Oak, more than 30ft (10m) in diameter, where Maid Marion and Robin pledged their undying love. There may be a heap of legend, folklore, tradition and just plain fibbing about the tales of this hero, but no one ever let that stop them having a good time. Just north of Sherwood Forest is an area known as the Dukeries, after the five dukes who owned much of the land. Here you will find **Clumber Park**, a wide expanse of parkland, peaceful woods, open heath and extensive farmland, worth visiting for its picnic sites and woodland paths. Clumber was once the home of the Dukes of Newcastle, and though the house was demolished in 1938, many features of the estate remain, including a splendid Gothic Revival chapel.

> ### DID YOU KNOW?
>
> According to a survey by the Arts Council of England, the Top 3 Shakespeare plays in tickets sold are *Macbeth*, *As you Like It* and *A Midsummer Night's Dream*.

Below: a *narrow alleyway in Shrewsbury*

✚ 54A2
ℹ The Square ☎ 01743 281200 🕐 May–Sep Mon–Sat 10–6, Sun 10–4; Oct–Apr, Mon–Sat 10–5; Easter Sun 10–4

SHREWSBURY ⊕⊕⊕

The River Severn determined Shrewsbury's siting, its development and its present character. The Saxon town of Scrobbesbyrig was built within a natural moat provided by a tight loop of the river, completely encircled except for a small gap – 'islanded in Severn stream', as A E Housman put it. Shrewsbury is the county town of Shropshire and claims to be the finest Tudor town in England. It's a crazy mish-mash of medieval streets, half-timbered buildings and modern shops. Among the town's most interesting buildings are the red sandstone abbey (just on the edge of town) and the Market Hall, opposite the information centre, built in 1596 for the sale of woollen cloth. But you'll find more intriguing places along Grope Lane, Butcher Row and around St Alkmund's Church. One of the town's more famous sons is Charles Darwin. He attended Shrewsbury School, a splendid building founded by Edward VI in 1552.

STOKE-ON-TRENT ✪✪

It is porcelain that justifies a visit to Stoke, an otherwise unattractive urban sprawl. Many of the world's most famous potteries developed here, thanks to the abundant presence of marl clay, coal, water, iron, copper and lead, the raw materials for the production of ceramics. Royal Doulton, Minton, Spode and Wedgwood all come from here. The city itself is an amalgam of six smaller towns – Stoke, Hanley, Tunstall, Longton, Burslem and Fenton. At the Gladstone Pottery Museum in Longton local crafts-people demonstrate the skills of producing pottery, and there are informative exhibits at the Royal Doulton Visitor Centre in Nile Street, Burslem, the World of Spode near the train station in Church Street, Stoke, the Wedgwood Visitor Centre in Barlaston, and the Potteries Museum in Bethesda Street, Hanley.

54B3
Quadrant Road, Hanley
☎ 01782 236000;
www.stoke.gov.uk
🕐 Mon–Sat 9:30–5.15

Above left: Anne Hathaway's Cottage, Stratford-upon-Avon
Above: Gladstone's Pottery Museum tells the story of Stoke-on-Trent

STRATFORD-UPON-AVON ✪✪

The birthplace of William Shakespeare (► 14), Stratford-upon-Avon is one of the busiest tourist attractions outside London. Aside from the extensive theatre complexes (► 113), you can visit the Bard's birthplace, a half-timbered Tudor house, now restored as a museum, and his wife Anne Hathaway's pretty thatched cottage in the nearby village of Shottery. The town itself is dominated by the Shakespeare legacy and most of its remaining medieval and Tudor buildings are given some significance in the playwright's life. Guided tours, on foot and by bus, are available. Ask at the tourist information centre for details.

54B2
Bridgefoot, near bus station ☎ 01789 293127; www.shakespeare-country.co.uk 🕐 Apr–Sep Mon–Sat 9.30–5.30, Sun 10.30–4.30; Oct–Apr Mon–Sat 9.30–5, Sun 10–3

❓ Royal Shakespeare Company ☎ Box Office 0870 609 1110; www.rsc.org.uk

TATTON PARK ✪✪

Tatton is one of the most complete historic estates to which the public has access. The Georgian Tatton Hall sits amid a landscaped deer park with woodland walks and bicycle trails, and is most opulently decorated, providing a fine setting for the Egerton family's collections of pictures, books, china, glass, silver and furniture manufactured by the Lancashire family, the Gillows. Victorian grandeur extends into the gardens where you''ll find Japanese and Italian themes, a rose garden and maze.

54A3
✉ Knutsford
☎ 01625 534400;
www.tattonpark.org.uk
🕐 House: Apr–Oct Tue–Sun 1–5. Park/gardens: Apr–Oct Tue–Sun 10.30–6/7; rest of year Tue–Sun 11–4/5
🍴 Restaurant (££)
♿ Good 🚫 Moderate

54B2
☎ 0870 4422000
🕐 Apr–Sep daily 10–6;
Oct–Mar 10–5
🍴 Café and restaurant
♿ Few
👋 Expensive

Below: *rowers are a*
regular sight on the River
Severn below Worcester
Cathedral

54B2
ℹ The Guildhall, High Street
☎ 01905 726311

WARWICK CASTLE ●●●

Hailed as the finest medieval castle in England, the sheer size of Warwick Castle has you well on the way to believing it. And though there is much in the claim, a sizeable chunk of the castle dates from 19th-century restoration which turned the castle into a magnificent stately home. It remains, nevertheless, a powerful and important piece of English architecture. The first 'castle' was Saxon, built in AD 914 by Ethelfleda, daughter of Alfred the Great. This was followed by a wooden Norman castle, then the 14th-century stone version which remains today. The best view is seen looking up from the town bridge.

WORCESTER ●●●

Worcester, on the River Severn, first attained prominence during Roman times, when a flourishing iron smelting industry and a port were established. Today, the city's glory is the cathedral, which has a history extending to AD 680, when a wooden cathedral is known to have existed. There are other interesting buildings around the cathedral. In particular, don't miss the 14th-century Edgar Tower, the Kings' School buildings in College Green, the Deanery, the Watergate, the Old Palace or the ruins of Guesten Hall. The Commandery building dates from the 15th century. It served as Charles II's headquarters for a time and now functions as an excellent museum devoted to the Civil War. For many, Worcester's fame rests on the manufacture here of Royal Worcester porcelain (and Worcestershire Sauce). The porcelain factory is not far from the river, between the cathedral and the suburb of Diglis.

Southwest England

The Southwest, also known as the 'West Country', reaches from Gloucester on the River Severn all the way to Land's End, and has some of the most naturally beautiful tracts of countryside anywhere in England. Here leafy lanes and flowering hedgerows pattern rolling green hills and link picture-postcard villages with thatched cottages, stately homes, riverside pubs and pre-historic sites that tell so much of England's heritage. The two great national parks – Dartmoor and Exmoor – provide wide, open spaces and the chance to escape and unwind, and these are supplemented by a string of Areas of Outstanding Natural Beauty. Above all, the Southwest is a land of rich pastures that produce some of the finest lamb, beef and pork, cheeses and milk, and is a top cider-producing area, able to boast cider of national and international reputation.

'The devil will not come to Cornwall for fear of being put in a pie.'

ANON.
Old Cornish Saying

●

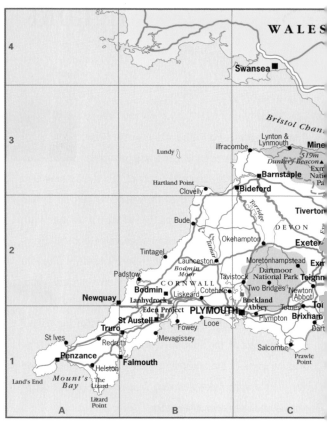

AVEBURY ●●●

The village of Avebury stands largely within a stone circle that rivals Stonehenge, though the individual stones are smaller. An enormous earthwork encloses the main circle, which is thought to have been built around 2500 BC. On first impressions it is difficult to grasp what Avebury is about, but this is partially rectified by the **Alexander Keiller Museum** at the west entrance to the site.

BATH (➤ 16, TOP TEN)

BRISTOL ●●●

Bristol ensured its place as an inland port to rival London from the Middle Ages, when its wealth grew on the triangular trade in slaves, cocoa, sugar, tobacco and manufactured goods between the New World and Africa. Many of the buildings from this period were damaged

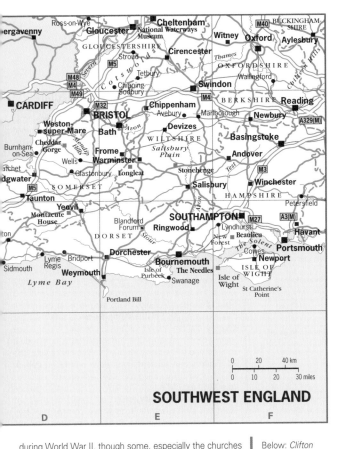

SOUTHWEST ENGLAND

during World War II, though some, especially the churches such as St Mary Radcliffe, remained intact.

In the 19th century, the engineer Brunel created two of the city's most famous monuments, the *SS Great Britain*, the world's first ocean-going steamship with screw propulsion, and the spectacular Clifton Suspension Bridge, a magnificent structure high above the Avon Gorge. The docks have been rejuvenated by developments and now offer eateries, family attractions and museums.

Below: *Clifton Suspension Bridge, Bristol*

66C2
Yelverton
01822 853607
Restaurant and tearoom
Good
Moderate

67D3

Cheddar Caves
01934 742343; www.
cheddarsomerset.co.uk
May–mid-Sep, daily 10–5;
mid-Sep–Apr, 10–4.30
Café and shops
Expensive

67E4
The Promenade
01242 522878; www.
visitcheltenham.gov.uk
Mon–Sat, 9:30–5:15

Pittville Pump Room
Pittville Park
01242 523852
Free

Art Gallery and Museum
Clarence Street
01242 237431
Free

Below: *Regency
architecture, like the
Pittville Pump Room, is a
dominant feature in
Cheltenham*

BUCKLAND ABBEY

Concealed in a secluded valley above the River Tavy,
Buckland used to be a small but prominent Cistercian
monastery. The house incorporates the ruins of the 13th-
century abbey church, and has strong connections with Sir
Francis Drake and his rival, Sir Richard Grenville.

CHEDDAR GORGE

Slicing through the Mendip Hills, this limestone gorge is an
impressive and beautiful natural phenomenon. The road
through the gorge runs for about 2 miles (3.2km), and at its
narrowest passes below cliffs almost 500ft (152m) high.
Beneath the gorge the **Cheddar Caves** were fashioned by
subterranean rivers during the last Ice Age, and were later
occupied by prehistoric man.

CHELTENHAM

The spa town of Cheltenham, well known for its racecourse
and its Ladies' College, is an excellent place from which to
explore the Cotswolds. Most visitors come here today for
the architecture rather than for the waters. The town suffers
from unimaginative planning that sprinkles shopping centres
in among attractive squares, gardens and elegant, Regency-
period buildings. Ironically, the civic offices are one of the
best features of Cheltenham, and a most delightful
thoroughfare. The **Pittville Pump Room**, a mile from the
town centre, in an area of villas and parkland, is one of the
town's finest examples of the Regency style, constructed
as a spa and social centre for Joseph Pitt's new estate. The
Art Gallery and Museum has sections covering William
Morris, the English craftsman, poet and socialist, and the
Arts and Crafts Movement, which sprang from his association with pre-Raphaelite colleagues. Lovers of music will
want to visit 4 Clarence Road where composer Gustav
Holst, best known for *The Planets*, was born. Displays
include Holst memorabilia and descriptions of life in the 19th
and early 20th century.

Left: *the gazebo in Cotehele House gardens*

COTEHELE HOUSE ⊘⊘

Leaning into the hillside above the River Tamar, Cotehele was mainly built between 1485 and 1627, and was, for centuries, the home of the Edgcumbe family. This is a small and fragile house; consequently visitor numbers are limited to 80 at any one time, so be prepared to wait for entry. The house contains tapestries and original furniture and armour, but if you have to wait, then the formal gardens, which overlook a beautiful valley garden, will agreeably pass your time.

⊞ 66B2
✉ St Dominick, near Saltash
☎ 01579 351346; 01579 352739 information line
⊙ House: Easter–Oct Sat–Thu 11–5 (Oct 11–4.30). Gardens: daily 10.30–dusk
¶¶ The Barn café (£)
♿ Good
▨ Moderate

THE COTSWOLDS (► 17, TOP TEN)

DARTMOOR ⊘⊘⊘

Wild, bleak, high and windswept, Dartmoor is the only true wilderness in southern England. It occupies the main part of the country between Exeter and Plymouth, and has a 'grim charm', alluded to by Sir Arthur Conan Doyle in *The Hound of the Baskervilles*. But it has a distinct beauty too, that should compel everyone to cross its barren moors at least once. That prehistoric man found it less forbidding is evidenced by the scattered remnants of Stone and Bronze Age presence. There are still remains to be found of tin and copper mining here, and the museum at **Morwellham Quay** is a fascinating place to learn about this aspect of the region's history. The moor has been a protected National Park since 1951.

⊞ 66C2

Dartmoor National Park
ℹ High Moorland Visitor Centre, Tavistock Road, Princetown PL20 6QF
☎ 01822 89041; www.dartmoor-guide.co.uk

Morwellham Quay
✉ Morwellham
☎ 01822 832766
♿ Some good parts
▨ Moderate

DORCHESTER ⊘⊘

For lovers of Thomas Hardy's works this is the place to visit, for he was born just three miles away at Higher Bockhampton. He worked as an architect in the town, and his novel, *The Mayor of Casterbridge*, describes the town as it was in the mid-19th century. The High Street is particularly handsome, and boasts a variety of Georgian town houses. The 18th-century Shire Hall contains the old county court, preserved as a memorial to the Tolpuddle Martyrs who were tried here in 1834. Nearby Maiden Castle is the largest pre-Roman earthwork in England.

⊞ 67E2
ℹ 11 Antelope Walk
☎ 01305 267992; www.westdorset.com
⊙ Summer Mon–Sat 9–5, Sun 10–3; winter Mon–Sat 9–4

Left: *Thomas Hardy was born not far from Dorchester and described many features of the town in* The Mayor of Casterbridge

Lizard

Distance
7½ miles (12km)

Time
5 hours with stops, 3–4 hours
without stopping

Start and End Point
Lizard lighthouse car park
✚ 66A1

Lunch
The Inn at Cadgwith (£–££)

A challenging walk through spectacular coastal scenery with lunch in a picturesque fishing village.

Head towards the lighthouse and soon go into the grounds of Polbrean Hotel, heading for the cliff path. Turn left along the path and follow it to Housel Bay. Continue round Bass Point.

The disused castellated building here was once a signal station.

At Kilcobben Cove go behind the lifeboat station and into Church Cove.

On the beach is a lifeboat station built at the end of the 19th century in such a way that the lifeboat had to be turned through ninety degrees before it could be launched; it didn't last.

Follow the coastal path to the Devil's Frying Pan, a large, collapsed cave, and go round the back of it to Inglewidden. Continue with the coastal path to Cadgwith, and go through the gardens of Hillside.

Cadgwith is a charming village on steep sea slopes, with lots of thatched cottages and buildings in the Serpentine rock for which the Lizard is famous.

Above: *Cadgwith, a charming village near The Lizard in Cornwall*

Go back up to Hillside, but turn right in Prazegooth Lane. At the top, bear right to a road. Turn left, pass Gwavas Jersey Farm and, when the road bends right, go forward onto a footpath. Head across a field to a marker pole, and up steps onto the top of a wall. At the other end gain a concrete farm access road to Trethvas Farm, and turn left for The Lizard. Continue now across fields to The Lizard, and then head for the 'Most Southerly Point'. In so doing you will return to your starting point.

EDEN PROJECT ✪✪✪

In a former clay quarry, this 37 acre (15ha) site is a floral and rainforest gateway into the world of plants. Inside the two gigantic 'biomes' – futuristic conservatories – climates of the world are re-created. Pathways wind through plants from places like the Amazon, West Africa, Malaysia, the Mediterranean, South Africa and California.

➕ 66B1
✉ Bodelva, St Austell
☎ 01726 811911;
   www.edenproject.com
🕐 Mar–Oct daily 10–6;
   Nov–Feb 10–4.30
🍴 Café 💷 Expensive
♿ Good

EXETER ✪✪✪

In spite of suffering extensive war damage, Exeter, the county town of Devon, retains much of its considerable charm and has a commanding position on the River Exe.

Today, the town's most distinguished feature is the cathedral, a superb architectural masterpiece enhanced by two great Norman towers that flank the nave. Inside you find the longest unbroken Gothic ceiling in the world, a stunning bishop's throne and splendid misericords that are thought to be the oldest in the country, dating from 1260.

➕ 66C2
ℹ Civic Centre, Paris Street
   ☎ 01392 265700;
   www.exeter.gov.uk
   🕐 Mon–Sat 9–5, Sun (in summer) 10–4

Below: *weavers' cottages and Georgian houses line the streets of Frome*

EXMOOR (➤ 18, TOP TEN)

FROME ✪✪

Lying at the eastern end of the Mendip Hills, Frome (pronounced 'froom') is a picturesque collection of steep cobbled streets, weavers' cottages, Georgian houses, old shops and a thriving market. The town's prosperity was founded on cloth making, chiefly from the medieval period to the end of the 18th century. Catherine Hill and Gentle Street are worth exploring and the congregational chapel on Rook Lane is particularly fine.

➕ 67E3
ℹ The Round Tower, Justice Lane ☎ 01373 467271
   🕐 Mon–Sat 10–5/4.30

GLASTONBURY ✪✪✪

Glastonbury was a centre of the early Christian church and lies at the heart of the mystical Isle of Avalon. Stories abound of the Holy Grail, King Arthur and the miraculous Glastonbury Thorn, said to have sprouted from the staff of Joseph of Arimathea. There are abbey ruins and a tower crowning the evocative Tor, a conical hill rising above the Somerset Levels, but the area is best known these days for the vast summer music **festival** at nearby Pilton. To the south, the Jacobean Montacute House, near Yeovil, displays important works from the National Portrait Gallery.

➕ 67D3
ℹ 9 High Street BA6 9DP
   ☎ 01458 832954; www.
   glastonburytic.co.uk
   🕐 Sun–Thu 10–5, Fri & Sun 10–5.30; sometimes closed 1–2
Glastonbury Festival
☎ 01749 890470

71

In the Know

If you only have a short time to visit England, or would like to get a real flavour of the country, here are some ideas:

10
Ways to Be a Local

Have lunch at a country pub – see opposite.

Visit a seaside resort, such as Mablethorpe on the east coast or Margate in Kent.

Shop at a large shopping complex like The Trafford Centre, Manchester, newly opened with lots of shops.

Visit a traditional street market – these are excellent places to go bargain hunting.

Left: *changing the guard at Horse Guards Parade*
Below: *Margate beach*

Have a picnic by a river or in a park, a relaxing way to enjoy a bite to eat.

Take a ride on the top deck of a double-decker bus – you get to see so much more.

Go to a car boot sale – these seem to appear everywhere, usually at weekends; you can pick up some real bargains.

See the changing of the guard at Horse Guards Parade, Whitehall, London.

Watch a village cricket match, and enjoy the relaxing atmosphere.

Be flexible – change your plans to suit your mood.

10
Good Places to Have Lunch

The Glass House (£–££)
✉ Rydal Road (next to Adrian Sankey's glass-blowing shop), Ambleside, Cumbria ☎ 015394 32137 Good range and inexpensive.

The Arcades (£–££)
✉ Victorian Quarter Harbour, Leeds. Try Ruskin's Tea Rooms or Café Arcade. Good variety at sensible prices.

Everyman Bistro (£–££)
✉ 5 Hope Street, Liverpool ☎ 0151 708 9545. Cheap, good food and delicious desserts.

Tamarind (££–£££)
✉ 20 Queen Street, London ☎ 020 7629 3561. Delhi meets Mayfair.

Tate Britain Restaurant (££)
✉ Millbank, London ☎ 020 7887 8000. Kill two birds with one stone.

Pump Room (££)
✉ Abbey Church Yard, Bath ☎ 01225 477785. Be serenaded by musicians as you have lunch or sip afternoon tea at this Georgian pump room.

Loch Fyne Restaurant & Oyster Bar (£–££)

✉ 17 King Street, Nottingham ☎ 01159 508 481. Excellent Scottish oyster and smoked seafood.

The Old Success Inn (£–££)

✉ Sennen Cove, Cornwall ☎ 01736 871232. Home-made specials, seafood, sandwiches.

The Refectory (£)

✉ Cathedral Cloisters, Wells. 18th-century monuments, atmospheric and cheap.

Brown's (££)

✉ South Quay, Worcester ☎ 01905 26263. Close by the Severn; sometimes in it.

10
Good Pubs

The New Inn

✉ Yealand Conyers, Lancashire.
An early 17th-century ivy-covered stone pub that is becoming especially popular for its imaginative blackboard 'specials'.

The Old Nag's Head

✉ Edale, Derbyshire.
At the start of the Pennine Way, this free house dates from 1577, when customers would include the drivers of packhorse teams.

The George Inn

✉ Hubberholme, Wharfedale, North Yorkshire.
A truly traditional Dales pub that reeks of character – white-washed walls, stone-flaggged floor, beamed ceilings, open fires and 18th-century charm.

The Ringlestone Inn

✉ Ringlestone, Kent.
An atmospheric 17th-century ale house on the top of the North Downs besides the Pilgrims Way.

Harrow Inn

✉ Steep, Hampshire.
Tucked away down a sleepy lane, this excellent, unspoilt country pub has been run by the same family since 1929.

The Britannia Inn

✉ Elterwater, Cumbria.
Everything you would expect from a traditional British inn. The Britannia stands next to a village green shared with an ancient maple tree.

The Lamb Inn

✉ Sheep Street, Burford, Oxfordshire. The unchanging character and atmosphere of this civilised 500-year-old inn appeals to everyone.

The Saracen's Head

✉ Wolterton, Erpingham, Norfolk. Norfolk Dining Pub of 1999, where originality and quality count most.

The George of Stamford

✉ 71 St Martin's, Stamford, Lincolnshire. A smart and busy old coaching inn built in 1597 for Lord Burghley.

Cott Inn

✉ Cott, Dartington, Devon. Warm, friendly with open fires, flagstones and polished brasses.

10
Top Activities

• Go to a major football match

Above: *the Fitzwilliam Museum, Cambridge*

• Go for a country walk
• Hire a boat and go rowing on a park lake or river
• Visit a cathedral
• Go horse riding
• Visit a major art gallery
• Go to a provincial orchestral concert
• Tour the country lanes on a hired bike
• Visit a stately home
• Go to an agricultural show

10
Best 'Heritage' Museums

• Flagship Portsmouth (➤ 75)
• Ironbridge Gorge (➤ 59)
• Kelham Island Museum, Sheffield (➤ 49)
• Killhope Lead Mining Centre, Co Durham (➤ 46)
• Morwellham Quay, nr Tavistock, Devon (➤ 69)
• National Coal Mining Museum England, Wakefield (➤ 48)
• National Waterways Museum, Gloucester (➤ 109)
• North of England Open Air Museum, Beamish, Co Durham (➤ 48)
• Quarry Bank Mill, Styal (➤ 62)
• Weald and Downland Open Air Museum, Singleton, West Sussex (➤ 90)

67E4
28 Southgate Street
☎ 01452 396572
🕐 Mon–Sat 10–5

GLOUCESTER ●●●

From Roman origins, Gloucester became a major port on the River Severn, until difficulties of navigation shifted the focus of trade to Bristol, substantially downstream. The docks, developed following the opening of the Sharpness Canal in 1827, declined too, but in recent years have seen a revival, and are now a vigorous and vast commercial enterprise, especially if you're looking for antiques. The pride of Gloucester, however, is its enormous cathedral, which has massive Norman columns, and the tomb of Edward II. Gloucester's lively streets are bustling with shops, pubs and businesses, but all in a noticeably lower key than at, say, nearby Cheltenham. Gloucester is very down to earth, and all the better for it.

67F2
Westridge Centre, Brading Road, Ryde PO33 1QS ☎ 01983 813800; www.islandbreaks.co.uk
🕐 Summer, daily 9–6 (Sat from 9:30); winter, daily 10–4

Osborne House
✉ 1 mile (1.6km) east of Cowes
☎ 01983 200022
💰 Expensive

ISLE OF WIGHT ●●

Known locally as 'The Island', the Isle of Wight packs a great scenic punch. It has a mild climate, and its remoteness, though it is only just off the Hampshire coast, has attracted many famous visitors, including Tennyson, Charles Dickens and Queen Victoria, who built a retreat for her family at **Osborne**, and lived here after Albert died. Not surprisingly then, the island has a good deal of Victoriana. The island has beautiful, unspoilt countryside much like Southern England without the traffic, and a varied and impressive coastline, with chalk stacks (the Needles – best seen as you approach by ferry from France) and sandy beaches.

66B2
✉ Lanhydrock, near Bodmin
☎ 01208 73320
🕐 House: Easter–Oct, Tue–Fri 11–5.30 (also holiday Mon). Gardens: mid-Feb–Nov daily 10–6; Nov–Feb dawn–dusk
🍴 Restaurant and café (£–££)
♿ Good
💰 Moderate

LANHYDROCK HOUSE ●●

Lanhydrock House is one of the most fascinating late 19th-century houses in England, full of period atmosphere and the trappings of a high Victorian country house. The gatehouse and north wing survive from the 17th century, but the rest of the house was rebuilt following a fire in 1881. The gardens are famously beautiful, with a superb collection of magnolias, rhododendrons and camellias.

Right: *one of the ornate bathrooms at Lanhydrock House, near Bodmin*

LONGLEAT

Longleat House is a vast Elizabethan mansion, with 19th-century interiors and numerous tourist attractions, not least lions, sea-lions, a railway and the world's longest hedge maze. The house has been the home of the Thynne (or Thynn) family for more than 450 years, and is now lived in by the 7th Marquess of Bath and his family. As well as providing visitor attractions, Longleat also plays an important role in the world programme of the breeding and conservation of endangered species.

67E3

✉ Warminster ☎ 01985 844400; www.longleat. co.uk

🕐 Park/attractions: Apr–Nov, daily 10–4/5. House: Apr–Sep 10–5.30; rest of year tours only

🍴 Cafés (£–££) 🚻 Good

💷 Expensive

Below: *Longleat House*

NEW FOREST

The name of this vast special heritage area in southwest Hampshire is misleading. There is more heathland than woodland and it certainly isn't new. It's the remains of a primeval forest enclosed and protected by William the Conqueror, who used it as a deer-hunting reserve. Forest people still graze their animals and exercise ancient woodland rights that go back to the time of the Conquest. The main wooded area is around Lyndhurst, the so-called 'capital' of the Forest. In the south of the forest lies Beaulieu, a pretty village, most famous for the **National Motor Museum,** with over 250 historic vehicles.

67F2

ℹ New Forest Visitor Information Centre, High Street, Lyndhurst ☎ 023 8028 2269; www.the newforest.co.uk 🕐 Mar–Jun, Sep–Oct Mon–Sun 10–5; Jul–Aug Mon–Sun 10–6; Nov–Feb Mon–Fri 10–4, Sat–Sun 10–5

National Motor Museum

✉ Beaulieu, Hampshire ☎ 01590 612345

PORTSMOUTH

Occupying the peninsula of Portsea Island, Portsmouth is Britain's foremost naval base. The Romans were not slow to recognise the strategic importance of this position, and built a fortress here. But it was only after the Norman Conquest that a peopled settlement developed, and not until Tudor times that the position was fully exploited. The Royal Naval Base in Queen Street is where you'll find the **Flagship Portsmouth,** comprising HMS *Warrior* 1860, HMS *Victory* and the *Mary Rose*, the Royal Naval Museum, the Dockyard Apprentice exhibition and the Warships by Water boat tour.

67F2

ℹ Clarence Esplanade, Southsea PO5 3PB ☎ 023 9282 6722; www. visitportsmouth.co.uk

Flagship Portsmouth

✉ Historic Dockyard ☎ 023 9286 1512

🕐 Apr–Oct daily 10–5.30; Nov–Mar 10–5

💷 Moderate

Dartmoor

Distance
65 miles (105km)

Time
2–3 hours, plus time for wandering

Start/end point
Tavistock
🞢 66C2

Lunch
Warren House Inn, Postbridge
(£–££)

The quiet lanes of Dartmoor are a delight on a clear day, but an awesome experience when the infamous moorland mists roll in.

Begin from Tavistock by taking the B3357 that heads eastwards onto the moors to the crossroads at Two Bridges, and from there turn left and shortly left again to follow the B3212. This change of direction now takes you northeast to the unspoilt market town of Moretonhampstead.

On the way you pass through Postbridge, where the largest and best preserved of Dartmoor's clapper bridges crosses the East Dart river. The bridge has been used by tin miners and farmers since medieval times.

In Moretonhampstead turn southeast on the A382 for Bovey Tracey, but don't actually go into the town. Instead, turn onto the B3387 for Haytor Vale and Widecombe in the Moor.

Above: *ancient clapper bridge, Postbridge, Dartmoor*

Widecombe in the Moor is a strong candidate for the most popular of Dartmoor's villages, set neatly in a hollow among granitic ridges. Widecombe is celebrated in a famous song, *Widdicombe Fair*, which features the fair, still held annually on the second Tuesday in September, but now mainly a tourist attraction.

From Widecombe winding lanes are followed to Dunstone, Ponsworthy and Dartmeet, where the East and West Dart rivers meet.

Right: *signpost, Widecombe Green*

The area around Dartmeet is lush and green, and only a few minutes' strolling is needed to get you away from the bustle of what is a very popular place.

From Dartmeet continue with the B3357, back to Two Bridges, but this time head southwest to Princetown, from where the B3212 will take you onto Yelverton and the A386, which returns you to Tavistock.

ISLE OF PURBECK ✪✪

Although not really an island, Purbeck certainly feels like one, jutting out into Poole Harbour. The best approach is by ferry from Sandbanks, from where the beautiful villages and the dramatic coastline can be explored quite easily on foot. Worth looking at are Wareham, Corfe Castle, Lulworth Cove and the limestone arch of Durdle Door. Swanage, the main town, is connected to Corfe by steam railway.

ST IVES ✪✪✪

Beautifully positioned, with sandy beaches flanking a rugged headland, St Ives is a small village of cobbled streets and steep alleyways. Its prosperity was founded on pilchards and tin mining, but now relies on tourism and art, having attracted many well-known artists including Barbara Hepworth, Naum Gabo and Roger Hilton. The **Barbara Hepworth Museum and Sculpture Garden** gives a detailed insight into the local arts scene. The **Tate Gallery**, overlooking the surfers on Porthmeor Beach, also shows local work. Opening times vary according to the season. A spectacular coastline continues southwest from here, with towering cliffs and boiling seas, reaching its most westerly point, and the most westerly in England, at Lands End.

SALISBURY ✪✪✪

England's finest cathedral city has grown since 1220, when the settlement moved from Old Sarum, an Iron-Age community just north of its present-day site. The cathedral, with its huge spire, was begun in 1220 and is entirely Early English in style. It is one of the finest medieval buildings in the country, and the Chapter House contains a copy of the Magna Carta. The city is a lovely mix of medieval, Georgian and Victorian buildings, a prosperous and important shopping centre and large market town, with no high-rise buildings to challenge the dominance of the cathedral.

STONEHENGE (▶ 23, TOP TEN)

🚩 67E2
ℹ️ The White House, Shore Road, Swanage ☎ 0870 4420680; www.dorset-info.co.uk 🕐 Daily 10–5. Closed Sun in winter

🚩 66A1
ℹ️ The Guildhall, Street-an-Pol ☎ 01736 796297; www.stives-cornwall.co.uk

Barbara Hepworth Museum and Sculpture Garden
✉️ Barnoon Hill
☎ 01736 796226
💷 Cheap

Tate Gallery
☎ 01736 796226
🍴 Café (£)
♿ Good
💷 Moderate

🚩 67E3
ℹ️ Fish Row ☎ 01722 334956 🕐 May, Mon–Sat 9.30–5, Sun 10.30–4.30; Jun–Sep, Mon–Sat 9.30–6, 10.30–4.30; Oct–Apr, Mon–Sat 9.30–5

Above: *interior of the Tate Gallery, St Ives*

🚹 66B1
ℹ️ Municipal Building,
Boscawen Street
☎ 01872 274555;
www.truro.gov.uk
🎫 Easter–May, Sep–Oct,
Mon–Fri 9-5:15, Sat
10–1; Jun–Aug, Mon–Fri
9–6, Sat 10-5;
Nov–Easter, Mon–Thu
9-5:15, Fri 9-5:45

TRURO   ✪✪

The county town of Cornwall was the main port for the export of tin, and became a medieval 'stannary' town, where tin was taken to be weighed and taxed. Little remains of Truro's ancient past, though there are numerous fine Georgian buildings, especially along Lemon Street. Completed in 1910, the cathedral was the first Anglican cathedral to be built since St Paul's in London, and incorporates parts of the earlier church that stood on the site.

🚹 67D3
ℹ️ Town Hall, Market Place
☎ 01749 672552; www.
wells-uk.com 🎫 Daily
Apr–Oct, 9:30–5:30;
Nov–Mar, 10–4

WELLS   ✪✪

The exquisite market place in this, England's smallest city, seems to have architecture from every conceivable period, including two medieval gatehouses, one of which leads to the splendid cathedral, the other to the Bishop's Palace.

The whole city seems to have altered little in 800 years, having successfully hung on to its medieval character, and is a perfect place to while away a relaxing day, or use as a base from which to visit the Mendip Hills and Cheddar Gorge (► 68).

The cathedral, one of England's most beautiful, dates from the 12th century, and its most impressive feature is the ornate west front, although many visitors are fascinated by the mechanical clock dating from 1392, high up in the north transept.

Above: *the Bishop's Palace in Wells, England's smallest city*

Cathedral Close is a cluster of attractive buildings with histories closely associated with the cathedral. A year-round programme of recitals provides the opportunity to hear a cathedral choir in full song (☎ 01749 674483).

🚹 67F3
ℹ️ Guildhall, The
Broadway
SO23 9LJ
☎ 01962
840500; www.
visitwinchester.
com
🎫 Mon–Sat
9.30–5.30, Sun
11–4, bank
holidays 10–4

WINCHESTER   ✪✪✪

Alfred the Great's Wessex capital was capital of all England from the 10th century until the Norman Conquest. It is one of the greatest historic cities in the country. 20 kings are buried here and it overflows with medieval and later buildings. So important was the city in the 11th century, that William the Conqueror's coronation was held both in London and Winchester. It was the monks of Winchester that he commissioned to carry out his Domesday Survey. The cathedral is one of the longest medieval buildings in the world and is reason enough to visit, but there are also the literary links. Jane Austen lived at nearby Chawton and died in the city in 1817, and pioneer angler Isaak Walton fished the local waters and also died here, in 1653.

Above: *Statue of Alfred the Great (presumably) in Winchester*

Southeast England

All along the south and east coasts of England, names and places ring significantly through the ages; along the White Cliffs of Dover and the Seven Sisters, cliff faces defiant against the sea and continental Europe, and through villages rich in the traditions of the sea. Here you can explore quiet cobbled streets or elegant waterfronts or enjoy winding cliff-top paths offering breathtaking views.

The southeast of England has always been the invader's route into the country and the landscape here bears testimony to this in its scars and monuments. '1066 country' embraces castles, battlefields and historic places, like Leeds Castle in Kent, home to Henry VIII, or the ancient city of Canterbury, destination of Chaucer's pilgrims. The richness of the countryside unfolds before you, and illustrates why the beautiful landscapes of Kent have earned it the epithet 'the Garden of England'.

> *'Our England is a garden that
> is full of stately views,
> Of borders, beds and shrubberies
> and lawns and avenues...'*

RUDYARD KIPLING
(1865–1936)

🏛 80C5
✉ Blickling, Norwich
☎ 01263 738030
🕐 House: Apr–Sep,
Wed–Sun 1–5; Oct 1–4.
Park: daily dawn–dusk
🍴 Restaurant and pantry
(£–££)
♿ Good
👐 Moderate

BLICKLING HALL

Built in the 17th century, red-brick Blicking Hall is one of England's great Jacobean houses, and famed for its spectacular long gallery, superb library and outstanding collection of furniture, pictures and tapestries. The gardens are splendid whatever the time of year, and the extensive surrounding parkland features a lake and many beautiful and relaxing walks. There are concerts in the summer and artists have included Simply Red and Van Morrison.

SOUTHEAST ENGLAND

BODIAM CASTLE ★★

Built in 1385, both as a defence and a home, Bodiam Castle is one of the most famous and evocative castles in Britain. The exterior is virtually complete and the ramparts rise dramatically above the moat. Enough of the interior survives to give an impression of castle life, and there are spiral staircases and battlements to explore. A small museum adds a social dimension.

✚ 80B2
✉ Robertsbridge, East Sussex
☎ 01580 830436
🕐 Vary seasonally
🍴 Tea room (£)
♿ Few
✋ Moderate

BRIGHTON ★★★

In the late 18th century the Prince of Wales, later George IV, visited Brighton and began the trend for seaside holidays. The seafront boasts elegant cream-coloured Regency terraces that extend to neighbouring Hove, but the city's most famous building is the extraordinary Indian-style Pavilion. Today, Brighton has become a bohemian city with a large student population and gay community and is known for its nightlife. For a glimpse of its roots and good shopping, head to The Lanes, a maze of narrow alleyways with interesting boutiques, antique shops, cafés and restaurants. North Laine, between the train station and The Lanes has pubs, cafés and more than 300 quirky shops selling 1950s kitsch.

✚ 80B1
ℹ 10 Bartholomew Square
☎ 01273 292590, 0906 7112255 (recording); www.visitbrighton.com
🕐 Jun–Sep, Mon–Fri 9–6:15, Sat 10–5, Sun 10–4; Oct–May, Mon–Sat 9–5, Sun 10–4

Below: *Brighton Pavilion was built as the seaside home of the Prince of Wales, later George IV*

BURY ST EDMUNDS ⭐⭐

🔲 80B4
ℹ 6 Angil Hill ☎ 01284
764667 ⏰ Easter–Sep,
Mon–Sat 9:30–5:30, Sun
11–4; Oct–Easter,
Mon–Fri 10–4, Sat 10–1

Bury's Norman grid street plan makes this attractive Suffolk town easy to explore. It takes its name from the 9th-century East Anglian king. Following his murder by Danish raiders, his bones were buried in the abbey and the town became a place of pilgrimage. The town, with the abbey ruins at its heart, became wealthy on the wool trade in the Middle Ages and is still a lively agricultural town today. Among its many attractive buildings are Moyse's Hall, now a local museum, but thought to be the oldest domestic property in East Anglia, and the Angel Hotel which features in *Pickwick Papers* by Charles Dickens.

CAMBRIDGE ⭐⭐⭐

🔲 80B4
ℹ Wheeler Street ☎ 0906
5862526; www.
tourismcambridge.com
⏰ Easter–Oct, Mon–Fri
10–6, Sat 10–5, Sun
11–4; Oct–Easter,
Mon–Fri 10–5:30, Sat
10–5

Fitzwilliam Museum
✉ Trumpington Street
☎ 01223 332900
⏰ Tue–Sat, 10–5, Sun
2:15–5
🖐 Free

Below: *King's College,
Cambridge*

Cambridge, and more particularly its world-renowned university, largely developed because of the persecution experienced by students at Oxford. They arrived in the 13th century and the University's oldest college dates from this time (Peterhouse, 1284). There are 31 colleges making up the modern University, the most recent being Robinson, added in 1977. Like Oxford (► 22), the town has benefited greatly from its academic connections. It is now the home of the 'Silicon Fen'– high-tech industries growing up in the boundless flatlands that surround the city. But the centre of Cambridge is all about its glorious buildings. King's College, famed for its magnificent 15th-century chapel and superb choir, forms one side of King's Parade. A climb up the tower of Great St Mary's Church, opposite, is rewarded with a view over the whole city. The oldest colleges, built around neat quadrangles, can easily be picked out. Further up a continuation of the same street stands Henry VIII's Trinity College. Between the colleges and the river lie the Backs, a series of genteel college gardens and lawns facing open fields across the water. You can hire the traditional punts to navigate the river. The biggest shopping area runs parallel to the colleges and is restrained in its modern use of the historic buildings. The botanic gardens and the outstanding collections in the **Fitzwilliam Museum** are also worth seeking out.

CANTERBURY ✪✪

Devastating bombing in World War II, during the so-called 'Baedeker Raids', did nothing to suppress the indomitable spirit of this historic old city, and many of the timber-framed buildings near the cathedral survived. Canterbury was a capital as long ago as Iron-Age times, and a major Roman town. In AD 597, St Augustine founded the monastery, Christ Church, which became the first cathedral in England. Its magnificent Gothic successor, largely dating from the 12th century, is Canterbury's greatest treasure. Thomas à Becket was brutally murdered here in 1170, and his shrine became one of the most popular in Europe, second only to Rome – a pilgrimage immortalised by Chaucer in *The Canterbury Tales* (1388). Today the Archbishop of Canterbury is the head of the Church of England and the leader of the worldwide Anglican community.

CHARTWELL ✪✪

The home of Sir Winston Churchill from 1924 until the end of his life, Chartwell is an unpretentious Victorian country house, with stunning views over the Weald, and it became the place from which Sir Winston drew inspiration. The rooms remain much as he left them, with pictures, maps and personal mementoes that strongly evoke the career and wide-ranging interests of England's wartime prime minister. The beautiful terraced gardens contain a pond and his garden studio in which many of his paintings can be seen.

CHILTERNS ✪✪

The Chilterns are a range of chalk hills extending in a curve from Dunstable in the north to Reading in the south, characterised by their beech woodlands and pretty villages. Fingest is the prettiest of these, nestling in wooded downland with a Norman church and 18th-century inn. The area has been well protected from the advances of London's suburbia, but remains extremely accessible from the capital, with fast train and tube links delivering you to the heart of this surprisingly quiet countryside. The western edge is marked by a chalkland ridge, traversed by the Ridgeway National Trail, itself following a prehistoric trade route, making excellent walking territory.

🔲 80C2

ℹ️ 12/13 Sun Street, The Buttermarket
☎ 01227 766567; www.canterbury.co.uk
🕐 Jan–Easter, Mon–Sat 10–4; Easter–Oct, Mon–Sat 9.30–5, Sun 10–4; Nov–Dec, Mon–Sun 10–4

Above: *the Buttermarket in Canterbury betrays nothing of the wartime devastation of the Baedeker raids*

🔲 80B2

✉️ Westerham, Kent
☎ 01732 866368 recorded information; 01732 86838
🕐 Jul–Aug, Tue–Sun & hols 11–5; late Mar–Jun, Sep–early Nov Wed–Sun & hols 11–5
🍴 Restaurant (£–££)
♿ Good
💷 Moderate

🔲 80A3

ℹ️ Paul's Row, High Wycombe ☎ 01494 421892; www.wycombe.gov.uk
🕐 Mon–Thu 9:30–5, Fri 9:30–4:30, Sat 9:30–4

Above: Dover Castle, a
formidable defensive
structure, was still used
as such in the 1980s

DOVER ✪✪

Dover is England's principal cross-channel port and reputedly the world's busiest passenger port. The spectacular **Dover Castle** is a formidable defensive structure, and used as such from the 12th century until the 1980s. Overlooking the town, it has a massive keep built by Henry II in the 1180s, with walls 17–22ft (5–7m) thick. During the Civil War, the castle was seized by Oliver Cromwell. It was further strengthened during the Napoleonic Wars and played an important role in World War II. The famous white cliffs are honeycombed with fortifications used during this conflict. Admiralty Lookout in the castle grounds is a great place for views of the cliffs and across the Channel. The proximity to German guns on the French coast earned the defences the title 'Hellfire Corner'. Dover Museum tells the story of the development of the town and port, and includes the Dover Bronze Age Boat, a gallery with information on the Bronze Age presented in many languages. The old harbour, which silted up, now lies beneath the modern town, and the existing harbour was built in the 19th century.

ELY ✪✪

Until the surrounding fens were drained, in the 17th century, the Isle of Ely was indeed an island, in the middle of a labyrinth of water-filled channels and overhanging foliage. So formidable a natural defence were the marshes, that those opposing the Norman invasion were able to do so until 1071. To mark their ultimate victory, the Normans built the massive 'Cathedral of the Fens', which towers above the low-lying land. Ely is an agreeable jumble of time-warped buildings dating from the 15th century to Georgian and Victorian times.

HASTINGS

Hastings is known to every schoolchild as the place where in 1066 the Norman Conquest of England began. By the time William of Normandy landed, Hastings was already a flourishing port. Today, it is a pleasing mixture of contemporary seaside resort, artists' retreat and a small fishing port. Look out for the tall weatherboarded fishing net stores, unique to the town. Understandably, Hastings makes the most of the '1066' story, as they do at nearby Battle, 5miles (8km) away, which boasts a magnificent abbey built to celebrate William's victory.

+ 80B1
i Queen's Square, Priory Meadow
☎ 01424 781111;
www.hastings.gov.uk
🕐 Jul–Sep, Mon–Sat 10–6, Sun 10–5; Oct–Jun, Mon–Sat 10–5, Sun 10–4:30

HEVER CASTLE

Once the home of Anne Boleyn, second wife of Henry VIII, and where Anne of Cleves, his fourth wife, lived after their divorce, Hever Castle is a fine, moated stronghold and contains many Tudor artefacts, paintings and other interesting objects. Having fallen into disrepair, the 13th-century castle was bought by William Waldorf Astor, the then American millionaire owner of *The Observer* newspaper, who had it painstakingly restored, and, though the Astor family no longer owns it, it remains a splendid example of regal life in Tudor times.

+ 80B2
✉ Hever, near Edenbridge, Kent
☎ 01732 865224;
www.hevercastle.co.uk
🕐 Mar and Nov, daily 11–4; Apr–Oct, daily 12–5 (gardens from 11)
🍴 The Moat and the Pavilion restaurants (£–££)
♿ Few 💷 Expensive

LEEDS CASTLE

Originally a Saxon royal manor built in AD 857, Leeds Castle, which in its present form was begun in 1120, became the home of the Norman Crevecouer family and later a royal palace during the reign of Edward I. The castle, which rises fairytale-like from a lake, has been the home of six medieval queens, and is a delightful place to visit. If you're travelling out from London Victoria, buy an all-inclusive rail ticket to Bearsted station, which includes coach shuttle and entry to the castle.

+ 80B2
✉ Leeds, near Maidstone, Kent
☎ 01622 765400;
www.leeds-castle.com
🕐 Apr–Oct, daily 10–5; Nov–Feb, daily 10–3. Closed 25 Dec
🍴 The Fairfax Hall (£–££) and The Terrace Room (££)
♿ Very good 💷 Expensive

LULLINGSTONE ROMAN VILLA

The villa was only discovered in 1939, and ranks as one of the major finds of the 20th century. It was built around AD 100, and was in use and extended throughout the Roman occupation. Much of the original villa's layout is visible, as are a number of mosaic floors.

+ 80B2
✉ Lullingstone Lane, Eynsford, Dartford, Kent
☎ 01322 863467
🕐 Late Mar–May, Aug–Sep daily 10–6; Oct 10–5; Nov–late Mar 10–4
🍴 Eynsford village
♿ Good
💷 Cheap

Left: *the incredible detail surviving in the mosaics, Lullingstone Roman Villa*

80C4
Station Road, Hoveton,
Wroxham ☎ 01603
782281

Below: *markets, like this
one at Norwich, are found
in most large English
towns*

80C4
The Forum, Millenium
Plain ☎ 01603 727927;
⊙ Mon–Sat 10–5:30/6,
Sun 10:30–4:30 (closed
Sun in winter)

80B2
✉ Penshurst, near
Tonbridge, Kent
☎ 01892 870307;
www.penhurstplace.com
⊙ Apr–early Nov, Sun–Fri
12–5:30, Sat 12–4; Mar
Sat 12–4, Sun 12–5:30
🍴 Garden Restaurant (£–££)
♿ Good
⊕ Moderate

80B2
95 High Street ☎ 01634
843666 ⊙ Mon–Sat
10–5, Sun 10:30–5

NORFOLK BROADS ●●●

Flowing through the heart of Norfolk is a spread of waterways known as 'The Broads', an area of slow-flowing rivers – the Yare, Waveney, Bure Ant and Thurne – and shallow lakes, 42 in all, that were created by the extraction of peat and subsequent flooding several hundred years ago. Sailing and cruising on the Broads are popular pursuits, and invariably pleasant ones; the wildlife on the Broads is second to none. The only efficient way of exploring the Broads is, of course, by boat, and you could easily spend many days here meandering around over 130 miles (200km) of lock-free, navigable waterways.

NORWICH ●●●

Whatever your interest the market city of Norwich has something to offer – architecture, art, museums, leisure activities or simply shopping. The slender-spired cathedral, surrounded by cobbled streets with fine old buildings, and the bustling, modern shopping centres are dominated by a

Norman castle, built around 1160, which itself houses a fine museum. Norwich is particularly well endowed with medieval churches (though not all are still in use), notably St John Maddermarket, which contains a fine collection of monumental brasses, 15th-century St Andrew's, and St Michael at Plea, which takes its name from the archdeacon's court. Undoubtedly a wealthy medieval city, Norwich is still East Anglia's unofficial capital, and is a useful base from which to explore the Broads and the beautiful Norfolk coastline.

PENSHURST PLACE ●●

The delightful village of Penshurst lies at the confluence of the rivers Eden and Medway and is dominated by 14th-century Penshurst Place. The finest privately owned manor house in Kent, it was birthplace of Sir Philip Sidney (1554–86), the English poet and Elizabethan soldier. The massive chestnut roof of the Barons Hall in Penshurst Place, built by Sir John de Pulteney, four times Mayor of London, is its most spectacular feature and the house is set in magnificent formal gardens.

ROCHESTER ●●

Rochester, known jointly with neighbouring Chatham as the Medway Towns, was founded by the Romans at the point where their great road from the Channel ports, Watling Street, crossed the River Medway. Later, in

AD 604, the Saxons founded a cathedral here, the second oldest in England, and one that was rebuilt by the Normans. They also built a fine castle here, recognising the city's strategic importance.

Many of the buildings in Rochester are Georgian and there is a pleasant intimacy about the place, which would have appealed greatly to novelist Charles Dickens, who knew Rochester well, and brought it into a number of his books, notably *Great Expectations*.

SAFFRON WALDEN ✪✪✪

This old market town's numerous timber-framed houses are a particular delight, many adorned with fine examples of the decorative plasterwork known as pargeting. There is a maze of medieval alleyways around the marketplace and book and antique shops along Church Street. Until the 18th century, this was the main centre for growing the saffron crocus and the wealth from the trade helped build the magnificent church of St Mary the Virgin.

🔲 80B3
ℹ️ 1 Market Place, Market Square ☎ 01799 510444
🕐 Apr–Oct, Mon–Sat 9:30–5:30; Nov–Mar, Mon–Sat 10–5

ST ALBANS ✪✪

According to tradition, Alban was a Roman soldier who converted to Christianity, and was tortured and beheaded because of his refusal to sacrifice to pagan gods. He became England's first Christian martyr, and the abbey, founded here by King Offa of Mercia in the 8th century on the site of his martyrdom, rose to be one of the wealthiest in the country. Its massive stone gateway still stands to the west of the cathedral.

St Alban's today is a thriving shopping and business centre, but it has always held an important position as a staging post on the highway to London from the north, and remains popular with visitors and pilgrims. To the south of the town, the **Gardens of the Rose**, with over 30,000 specimens, is the world's largest rose collection.

🔲 80A3
ℹ️ Town Hall, Market Place ☎ 01727 864511; www. stalbans.gov.uk
🕐 Mon–Sat 9:30–5:30, Sun 10:30–4:30; winter Mon–Sat 10–4

Gardens of the Rose
☎ 01727 850461
🕐 Jun–Sep, Mon–Sat 10–5, Sun, 10–6
🍴 Café (£–££) ✋ Moderate

Below: *timber-framed houses, Saffron Walden*

South Downs

Distance
55 miles (88km)

Time
2–3 hours plus stops

Start/end point
Chichester
⊞ 80A1

Lunch
You're spoiled for choice;
there are country pubs in
Chilgrove, South Harting,
Elsted, Lower Elsted,
Easebourne, Midhurst,
Cocking and West Dean

*Leave Chichester by heading north on the A286
for Midhurst, but just after Mid Lavant turn
onto the B2141, following a delightful route
through wooded downland to Chilgrove and
South Harting.*

Chilgrove is little more than a handful of cottages and a
pub in a richly green valley, dotted with isolated farms;
there are the remains of two Roman villas near by.

*Just as the B-road leaves South Harting, turn
right onto a minor road to East Harting, Elsted
and Lower Elsted and, ultimately, meet the
A272 at Stedham Common. Turn right and
shortly left for the hamlet of
Iping, where you cross the River
Rother.*

Iping is an attractive Downs village of
old cottages, a mill and a five-arched
bridge spanning the river. Stedham
Common is scattered with prehistoric
tumuli.

*A short way further on, turn
right and follow country lanes
towards Easebourne. When you
meet the A286, turn right and
go into Midhurst.*

Above: Cissbury Ring,
South Downs dates from
about 300 BC

Midhurst is a busy market town with a wide, spacious
North Street that contains many attractive buildings,
including a couple of fine pubs, one of which – the Angel –
is said to have been patronised by the Pilgrim Fathers.

*In the centre of Midhurst, where the road makes
a pronounced bend, look for the turning, on the
right, to Bepton and follow this to a T-junction,
near the hamlet. Turn left to Cocking, a
roadside village in a wooded gap. Continue to
follow the A286, first to West Dean, a lovely
place with lots of flint cottages.
From West Dean, stay on the main road to
return to Chichester.*

SEVEN SISTERS ✪✪

The country park that includes the famous landmark, the Seven Sisters, provides some of the finest coastal and riverside walking in the country, notably along the serpentine River Cuckmere into which the Seven Sisters finally slip. The Seven Sisters themselves are a stunning switchback of vertical chalk cliffs between Cuckmere Haven and Birling Gap.

SUFFOLK COAST AND HEATHS ✪✪

From its gently curving beaches to expansive wild heaths, reedbeds and wide estuaries, the Suffolk Coast and Heaths Area of Outstanding Natural Beauty is a stunning but fragile landscape. It extends roughly from Kessingland in the north to Aldeburgh, and is typical of the very best countryside of southeastern England. The coast is especially treasured for its wealth of wildlife and there is a splendid marshland bird reserve at Minsmere between Southwold and Leiston. On a different tack, Aldeburgh is famed for its annual festival of music and arts (Box Office: ☎ 01728 687110), begun in 1948 by composer Benjamin Britten and tenor Peter Pears, and held in June at Snape Maltings, 3 miles (5km) inland.

WALMER CASTLE ✪✪

Intended to withstand the assaults of the French and Spanish following Henry VIII's break with the Roman Catholic Church, Walmer Castle has an original design (gunpowder had suddenly become a new threat) that was low and squat with massively thick walls. Later the castle was transformed into a stately home and became used as the residence of the Lord Warden of the Cinque Ports; the current Lord Warden is the Queen Mother, who succeeds such eminent people as Pitt the Younger, the Duke of Wellington and Sir Winston Churchill.

✚ 80B1
ℹ Seven Sisters Country Park, Exceat, Seaford, East Sussex ☎ 01323 870280 ◷ Easter–Oct, Mon–Fri 10:30–4:30, Sat, Sun 10:30–5; Nov–Easter, weekends only 11–4

✚ 80C4

Above: *magnificent coastal scenery at the Seven Sisters in East Sussex*

✚ 80C2
✉ Kingsdown Road, Walmer, Kent
☎ 01304 364288
◷ Apr–Sep daily 10–6; Oct 10–5, Nov, Dec & Mar Wed–Sun 10–4; Jan & Feb Sat–Sun 10–4; closed 24–26 Dec and 1 Jan
🍴 Tearoom (£–££)
♿ Good 👟 Moderate

WEALD ⭐⭐

A varied and fascinating landscape between the chalkland scenery of the North and South Downs. Its name comes from the Old English word for woodland; the whole area was densely forested during Anglo-Saxon times. It became important for iron production before the industrial revolution, but today is peaceful farmland and forestry. The **open air museum** at Singleton is England's leading museum of historic buildings and traditional rural life.

WINDSOR ⭐⭐⭐

The handsome market town of Windsor boasts the largest castle in England, within the bounds of which is something approaching another small, walled town. The attractive streets, many of them cobbled, have numerous Georgian and timber-framed houses, and an outstanding Guildhall, designed by Sir Christopher Wren. The town is, of course, dominated by **Windsor Castle**, which is still occupied by the Queen. Work started on the castle in the 11th century, though most of the buildings are 12th century and altered both in the 19th century, and in the 20th, following a disastrous fire in 1992. Across the River Thames, Eton is home to the famous and exclusive Eton School, which counts prime ministers, kings and princes among its old boys.

Right: *the Round Tower, first built in wood by William the Conqueror, dominates Windsor Castle*

WOBURN ABBEY ⭐⭐⭐

Home of the Marquess of Tavistock, the palatial 18th-century mansion of Woburn Abbey contains one of the finest private collections in England of works of art by Van Dyck, Canaletto, Gainsborough, Rembrandt, Reynolds and Velazquez, as well as some exquisite porcelain, including the Sevres Gift Service presented to the 4th Duchess by Louise XV of France. A large part of the house's extensive parkland is given over to the Woburn Safari Park, the largest drive-through wildlife reserve in Britain, and only accessible by car.

Where To...

Above: *the Palace Pier, Brighton*
Right: *the man on the beat, a British 'bobby'*

London

Price rating

Approximate price for a three-course meal per person, excluding drinks:

£ = under £20
££ = £20–£30
£££ = over £30

Afternoon Tea

It is a popular myth, maintained wherever tourists are found, that afternoon tea is still an integral part of English life. It isn't, but if you want to take afternoon tea in style try one of the following London hotels: the Ritz, the Savoy, the Lanesborough, Le Meridien Waldorf (where you are serenaded by a harpist), Claridges or the Dorchester. It will be an expensive, but memorable, experience. Dress smartly (jacket and tie for men) and skip lunch beforehand. Slightly cheaper, but still classy, are Sotheby's and Fortnum & Mason.

Alastair Little Soho (£££)

Distinctive, stylish décor and light modern-European cooking are the hallmark here; booking well in advance is advised.

✉ 49 Frith Street, Soho ☎ 020 7734 5183 🕔 Lunch Mon–Fri 12–3; dinner Mon–Sat 6–11:30 🚇 Leicester Square, Tottenham Court Road

Blakes Dining Room (££)

Close by Camden Market, Blakes offers a varied and interesting menu from wide-ranging cuisines across the world.

✉ 31 Jamestown Road ☎ 020 7482 2959 🕔 Daily lunch, dinner 🚇 Camden Town

Blues Bistro and Bar (£–££)

A trendy but not too trendy bistro and bar with a small and pleasant dining room serving American/European food at reasonable prices.

✉ 42–43 Dean Street ☎ 020 7494 1966 🕔 Mon–Fri lunch, dinner, Sat, Sun dinner 🚇 Piccadilly Circus

Café-in-the-Crypt (£)

This tranquil oasis in the very heart of London lies beneath the Church of St Martin-in-the-Fields on the edge of Trafalgar Square, and provides good salads, soups, sandwiches and light meals.

✉ Duncannon Street, Trafalgar Square ☎ 020 7839 4342 🕔 Sun–Wed 10–8, Thur–Sat 10–11 🚇 Charing Cross, Leicester Square

Café Pacifico (£)

A long-established Mexican joint, but a cut above the average, and ideal for a break.

✉ 5 Langley Street ☎ 020 7379 7728 🕔 Daily 12–12 🚇 Covent Garden

Chez Gérard at the Opera Terrace (££)

A glass conservatory on top of Covent Garden's market provides a completely different atmosphere. A surprisingly good place for steak and chips.

✉ First Floor, Opera Terrace, Covent Garden Central Market ☎ 020 7379 0666 🕔 Mon–Sat 11AM–11:30pm, Sun 11–10:30 🚇 Covent Garden

Gay Hussar (££)

London's favourite East European restaurant serving good value, old-fashioned Hungarian food, and the haunt of literary, musical and Bohemian types. Still going strong after more than 50 years.

✉ 2 Greek Street ☎ 020 7437 0973 🕔 Lunch and dinner Mon–Sat 🚇 Tottenham Court Road

Gordon Ramsay (£££)

Some would say the best place in London to eat; certainly this is one of London's finest. The highest standards of cuisine, prepared with imagination and flair. Booking essential, but only taken up to a month in advance.

✉ 68 Royal Hospital Road ☎ 020 7352 4441 🕔 Mon–Fri lunch, dinner 🚇 Sloane Square

Livebait (££)

Award-winning fish and seafood restaurant serving whelks, prawns, crab and oysters. Booking essential to be sure of a table. Handy for the Old Vic theatre.

✉ 43 The Cut, Waterloo ☎ 020 7928 7211 🕔 Daily 12–3, 5:30–11:30; closed Sun 🚇 Waterloo

River Café (£££)
Famous advocates of regional Italian cooking, the River Café set new standards with familiar Italian ingredients.
✉ **Thames Wharf Studios, Rainville Road** ☎ **020 7386 4200** 🕐 **Mon–Sat lunch, dinner, Sun lunch** 🚇 **Hammersmith**

Rock and Sole Plaice (£)
This long-established 'chippie' is ideal for a late evening snack if you're in the Covent Garden area.
✉ **47 Endell Street** ☎ **020 7836 3785** 🕐 **Mon–Sat 11:30–12, Sun until 10/11** 🚇 **Covent Garden**

Rules (£££)
London's oldest restaurant, opened in 1798. Patronised by Charles Dickens, and Edward VII and Lillie Langtry, and serves top-quality British food. Winner of the 'Best British Food Award' 2003.
✉ **35 Maiden Lane, Covent Garden** ☎ **020 7836 5314** 🕐 **Mon–Sat 12–11:30, Sun 12–10:30** 🚇 **Covent Garden**

Soho Spice (££)
Probably the best value of all the Indian restaurants in Soho. Has a limited menu but the quality is very high.
✉ **124–126 Wardour Street** ☎ **020 7434 0808** 🕐 **Mon–Sat 11:30–12:30** 🚇 **Leicester Square, Tottenham Court Road**

Pubs
The Bricklayers Arms (£)
One of a clutch of traditional real ale pubs, to the north of bustling Oxford Street. Always a welcome haven from the shopping crowds.
✉ **Gresse Street** ☎ **020 7636 5593** 🕐 **Mon–Fri 11–11, Sat 12–11, Sun 12–10:30** 🚇 **Tottenham Court Road**

Moon under Water
A breathtaking conversion of the old Marquee Club, this fiercely modern restaurant has quickly established itself as one of the most popular around Charing Cross, attracting Soho trendies, students and tourists, as well as the after-work crowd.
✉ **Charing Cross Road** ☎ **020 7287 6039** 🕐 **Mon–Sat 10–11, Sun 12–10:30** 🚇 **Tottenham Court Road, Leicester Square**

The Old Bank of England
Splendidly converted austere Italianate building was until the mid-1970s a branch office of the Bank of England. The opulent bar never fails to impress, but screens in the spacious room create a delightfully intimate feel.
✉ **194 Fleet Street** ☎ **020 7430 2255** 🕐 **Mon–Fri 11–11 (until 8 Fri and 9 Mon–Thu)** 🚇 **Chancery Lane**

The Old Coffee House
Piled high with bric-a-brac, this pub is filled with an intriguing jumble of nostalgic ephemera, and serves good value bar food, too.
✉ **49 Beak Street** ☎ **020 7437 2197** 🕐 **Mon–Sat 11–11, Sun 12–3 and 7–10:30** 🚇 **Oxford Circus, Piccadilly Circus**

Prospect of Whitby
London's quintessential riverside pub was built in 1520. Famously patronised by, among others, Charles Dickens and the painters Turner and Whistler.
✉ **57 Wapping Wall** ☎ **020 7481 1095** 🕐 **Mon–Sat 11:30–11, Sun 12–10:30** 🚇 **Wapping**

Northern England

Harry Ramsden's

This is an institution in the great British fish and chip world. Based originally at Guiseley, near Leeds, Harry Ramsden's food emporia are spreading through England (and abroad, for that matter) at an alarming rate. A bit pricey for fish and chips (takeaways are cheaper), but an experience to be tried at least once – don't forget the pot of tea and bread and butter, and try making a chip butty!

Bettys of Harrogate (££)

For the ultimate tea room experience you can do little better than this bastion of traditional style. There are also branches in Northallerton, Ilkley and York.
✉ 1 Parliament Street, Harrogate, North Yorkshire ☎ 01423 502746 🕓 Daily 9–9

Darbar (£–££)

The multi-ethnic population in Leeds ensures the city has an abundance of Asian and Indian restaurants. This city-centre establishment is probably one of the best.
✉ 16–17 Kirkgate, Leeds ☎ 0113 246 0381 🕓 Mon–Sat lunch, dinner

Gianfranco (£–££)

A long-established Italian restaurant that is much better than the standard, run-of-the-mill, and with some attractive lunchtime and 'happy hour' menus.
✉ 6–10 Leazes Park Road, Newcastle upon Tyne ☎ 0191 222 0659 🕓 Daily lunch, dinner

The Inn at Whitewell (££)

Tremendously popular and beautifully set in the Forest of Bowland, the inn, a friendly country house, is surrounded by rolling wooded hills, high moors and green pastures.
✉ Whitewell, Forest of Bowland, Lancashire ☎ 01200 448222 🕓 Daily lunch, dinner

The Naz Brasserie (£–££)

Located just a few minutes from junction 29 on the M6, the Naz serves conventional English-Indian cuisine, but does a fine line in Bangladeshi and chef's specialities that give it the edge over less adventurous Indian restaurants.
✉ Club Street, off Station Road, Bamber Bridge, Preston, Lancashire ☎ 01772 626695 🕓 Mon–Fri 12:30–2, 6–11:30, Sat–Sun 12–12

St William's College Restaurant (££)

Candlelight and jazz, and a historic building next to the Minster, make this one of York's most popular eating places; mainly modern British with Mediterranean influences.
✉ 3 College Street, York ☎ 01904 634830 🕓 Mon–Sat lunch, dinner until 10, Sun lunch only

Sharrow Bay (£££)

Among the top places to eat in the Lake District, the Sharrow Bay is an experience in itself, best enjoyed by booking yourself in for a couple of nights and letting the atmosphere take over.
✉ Sharrow Bay, Howtown, Cumbria ☎ 017684 86301 🕓 Daily lunch, dinner. Closed Dec–late Feb

Simply Heathcote's (£££)

Stylish and sophisticated, minimalist eaterie serving modern British cuisine.
✉ Beetham Plaza, 25 The Strand, Liverpool ☎ 0151 236 3536 🕓 Daily lunch, dinner

Village Bakery (£)

Award-winning organic bakery and café in a converted barn overlooking the village green, at the foot of the Pennines. Breakfasts are large and splendid.
✉ Melmerby, near Penrith, Cumbria ☎ 01768 881515 🕓 Mon–Sat 8:30–5, Sun 9:30–5. Check for winter opening

Central England

Chez Jules (££)
This decent French restaurant in the busy centre of Birmingham does an excellent line in lunchtime specials.

✉ **5a Ethel Street, Birmingham** ☎ **0121 633 4664** 🕐 **Daily lunch, dinner; closed Sun dinner**

The Eagle and Child (£)
Access to this pub is through the reception of the Royalist Hotel, the oldest inn in England. It serves traditional English food and a good selection of real ales.

✉ **Stow on the Wold** ☎ **01451 830670** 🕐 **All day**

The George (£)
Overlooking a green fringed by trees, and on the edge of delectable Dovedale, The George is the focal point of a very pretty village. Cosy bars and a dining room with low beamed ceilings, or outside tables in warm weather, make this a popular pub/restaurant; a homely touch is that you order your meals at the kitchen door.

✉ **Alstonefield, Derbyshire** ☎ **01335 310205** 🕐 **Daily lunch, dinner**

King Charles II (££)
Although the 17th-century ambience is slightly contrived, the King Charles II nevertheless serves outstanding traditional English food.

✉ **New Street, Worcester** ☎ **01905 22449** 🕐 **Mon–Sat lunch, dinner**

The Opposition (££)
The best value in a food-laden street, serving imaginative international cuisine in a buzzing atmosphere; for something special, check out the dishes of the day listed on a board outside.

✉ **13 Sheep Street, Stratford-upon-Avon** ☎ **01789 269980** 🕐 **Daily lunch, dinner**

Oscar's (£–££)
In the same building as the tourist information centre, Oscar's serves excellent value-for-money meals, and outstanding pizzas with inclusive help-yourself salads. Always busy, but an ideal place to eat if you're exploring Shrewsbury.

✉ **The Square, Shrewsbury** ☎ **01743 281268** 🕐 **Daily lunch**

Rose and Crown (£–££)
A fine town centre inn, good for an all-day range of inexpensive bar meals and snacks.

✉ **Market Place, Warwick** ☎ **01926 411 117** 🕐 **All day**

Shimla Pinks (££)
City centre Indian restaurant with an open-style kitchen.

✉ **214 Broad Street, Birmingham** ☎ **0121 6330366** 🕐 **Mon–Fri 12–3, 6–11, Sat–Sun 3–11:30**

Teppanyaki (££)
Birmingham's first Japanese restaurant has a rising reputation for excellent and authentic food.

✉ **Arcadian Centre, Hurst Street, Birmingham** ☎ **0121 622 5183** 🕐 **Mon–Fri lunch, dinner, Sat dinner**

Ye Olde Trip to Jerusalem (£–££)
Very old pub, dating back to the 12th century, which is built into a rockface.

✉ **1 Brewhouse Yard, Castle Road, Nottingham** ☎ **0115 9473171** 🕐 **Daily 11–11**

Chain Eating
Throughout the length and breadth of England there is a vast network of chain eateries, some pub/hotel based, others catering for motorists or people in a hurry. They include Little Chef, Happy Eater, Burger King, the ubiquitous McDonald's, Brewers Fayre inns, Pizza Hut and Pizza Express. You'll find a lot of smaller, family run restaurants and cafés in just about every town you visit.

Southwest England

Seafood

Largely surrounded by, or not far from, water, it is inevitable that many of the restaurants and pubs in the Southwest specialise in seafood. Think of fresh, succulent lobsters, crawfish and crab straight from the pots and sea bass from the coastal waters, and you're on the right lines. But it isn't all seafood; the West Country farms produce some of the best raw materials for chefs to work with in the world.

Castle Hotel (£–££)

The Castle is something of a gastronomic institution in Somerset, and its 800-year history makes it the West Country's most enduring 'watering hole'. For something quick, try the BRAZZ, The Castle's lively brasserie.

✉ **Castle Green, Taunton, Somerset** ☎ **01823 272671** ⏱ **Daily lunch, dinner**

Le Champignon Sauvage (££–£££)

Classic cooking from David Everitt-Matthias in his delightful blue and yellow-painted restaurant

✉ **Suffolk Road, Cheltenham** ☎ **01242 573449** ⏱ **Tue–Sat lunch, dinner**

George & Dragon (££)

Award-winning pub specialising in fresh fish. National winners of the 1999 AA 'Best Seafood Pub'.

✉ **High Street, Rowde, Wiltshire** ☎ **01380 723053** ⏱ **Tue–Sat lunch, dinner**

The Moody Goose (£)

A small, elegant restaurant in the heart of the city; the owners have a passion for the seasonal produce of Britain.

✉ **7A Kingsmead Square, Bath** ☎ **01225 466688** ⏱ **Mon–Sat lunch, dinner (closed 2 weeks Jan)**

Riverside Restaurant (£–££)

A highly-regarded seafood restaurant in the heart of the fishing village of West Bay. Vegetarian and other dishes available. Booking strongly advised.

✉ **West Bay, Bridport, Dorset** ☎ **01308 422011** ⏱ **Lunch Tue–Sun; dinner Tue–Sat. Closed Dec–Feb**

Riverstation (££)

The conversion of the old river police station on the docks near Bristol's city centre has produced a light and airy building which houses a fine restaurant on the first floor and a deli/espresso bar at dock level, with balconies over the water.

✉ **The Grove, Bristol** ☎ **0117 914 4434** ⏱ **Deli: meals all day; restaurant: lunch, dinner daily**

Savery's at Karslake House (££–£££)

The spacious restaurant in this 15th-century malthouse quickly gained recognition among discerning eaters; set in charming countryside amid the peace and quiet of the Exmoor National Park.

✉ **Halse Lane, Winsford, Exmoor, Somerset** ☎ **01643 851242** ⏱ **Tue–Sat dinner (non-residents Fri–Sat only)**

The Seafood Restaurant (£££)

Rick Stein's popular restaurant is the place to go for inventive seafood; set price meals are value-for-money. Non-fish eaters need not fear, though that really is the reason for going.

✉ **Riverside, Padstow, Cornwall** ☎ **01841 532700** ⏱ **Lunch, dinner Mon–Sun**

Tanners Restaurant (££)

A historic 15th-century house where Pilgrim fathers ate their final meal in England. The modern menu has French and American influences.

✉ **Prysten House, Finewell Street, Plymouth** ☎ **01752 252001** ⏱ **Lunch, dinner Tue–Sat**

Southeast England

Augustine's (££)
Popular restaurant in the centre of town serving modern European cuisine.
✉ 1 and 2 Longport, Canterbury, Kent ☎ 01227 453063 🕐 Daily lunch, dinner; closed Sun dinner

The Crooked Barn (££)
Described as Oulton Broad's hidden oasis, this 18th-century thatched barn is a magnificent place to dine. The style of cuisine is 'New World' with excellent set menu lunches.
✉ Ivy House Farm Hotel, Ivy Lane, Oulton Broad, Lowestoft, Suffolk ☎ 01502 501353 🕐 Daily lunch, dinner

De La Pole Arms (££)
A delightful village pub, where the specialities include fish and chips in St Peter's wheat beer batter, or a seafood bowl.
✉ Wingfield (near Diss), Suffolk ☎ 01379 384545 🕐 Daily lunch, dinner; closed Mon in winter

Mortimer's on the Quay (£–££)
This splendid seafood restaurant offers a fine selection of dishes and daily specials, all served in a straightforward manner, which allows the freshness of the fish to speak for itself.
✉ 2 Duke Street, Ipswich ☎ 01473 230225 🕐 Mon–Sat lunch, dinner; closed Sun & hols

The Old Fire Engine House (££)
Owned and run by the same family for 30 years, this is an 18th-century building opposite St Mary's Church, and has a large walled garden and informal atmosphere. The cooking is based on local ingredients and classic English dishes.
✉ 25 St Mary's Street, Ely, Cambridgeshire ☎ 01353 662582 🕐 Mon–Sat lunch, dinner, Sun lunch; closed 2 weeks Xmas and hols

The Orangery (£££)
Modern English cooking served intelligently and with skill in a delightful Georgian setting. Eating here gives a distinct feeling of being in a typical country home.
✉ Congham Hall Country House Hotel, Grimston (near King's Lynn), Norfolk ☎ 01485 600250 🕐 Daily lunch, dinner

Tatlers (££)
Brasserie-style restaurant in a converted Georgian townhouse serving modern British cuisine with a French flavour.
✉ 21 Tombland, Norwich ☎ 01603 766670 🕐 Mon–Sat lunch, dinner

Terre á Terre (££)
Exciting vegetarian restaurant in the centre of Brighton with organic wine and beer also on the menu.
✉ 71 East Street, Brighton, E Sussex ☎ 01273 326688 🕐 Daily lunch, dinner; closed Mon lunch, 24–26 Dec, 1 Jan

The White Hart (£–££)
Built in 1505, the timbered exterior is matched by a heavily beamed interior with four fireplaces. Gardens run along both sides of a stream. Run by a partnership of chefs who each serve the highest quality food in an informal atmosphere.
✉ Great Yeldham, Halstead, Essex ☎ 01787 237250 🕐 Daily lunch, dinner

Lincolnshire Food
Lincolnshire is known for excellent sausages and fish. The port of Grimsby is one of the biggest fish markets in the country, and there are traditional smoke-houses, too, working with methods handed down from generation to generation. Also from the Fens comes soft fruit – raspberries, strawberries, blackcurrants and redcurrants, and gooseberries. Pick your own, or buy them from roadside stalls.

London

Hotel Prices

All prices are for one night's double room, whatever the occupancy – though it is rare for a whole family to be allowed to share

£ = £45–£70
££ = £70–£150
£££ = over £150

On a Budget

Travellers on a wafer-thin budget should consider staying at one of London's numerous YMCA/YWCA hostels or at one of the youth hostels. The YHA hostels in particular are extremely good value and in surprisingly central locations; consequently you'll need to book months ahead for the summer. Contact the Barbican YMCA ☎ 0207 6280697; www. ymca.org.uk, and the YHA ☎ 0870 770 8868; www.yha.org.uk.. London Tourist Board offices can help with other student, youth and group accomodation.

Athenaeum (£££)

This elegant hotel overlooking Green Park remains one of the most popular and friendly in London. Lovely bedrooms and a spa.
⊠ 116 Piccadilly ☎ 020 7499 3464 🚇 Green Park

Avonmore Hotel (££)

A privately-owned, award-winning B&B with just nine bedrooms and a friendly atmosphere.
⊠ 66 Avonmore Road, Kensington ☎ 020 7603 3121 🚇 West Kensington

Byron Hotel (££)

A charming, terraced house, thoughtfully restored. Bedrooms are comfortable and tastefully furnished.
⊠ 36–38 Queensborough Terrace ☎ 020 7243 0987 🚇 Queensway, Bayswater

Comfort Inn Hampstead (££)

Friendly hotel close to Hampstead Heath; popular with overseas visitors. Bedrooms well-equipped, and the public rooms are bright and cheerful.
⊠ 5–7 Frognal, Hampstead ☎ 020 7794 0101 🚇 Finchley Road

Comfort Inn Kensington (££)

Very conveniently located for Earl's Court, this cheerful modern hotel offers smart bedrooms and friendly service.
⊠ 22–32 West Cromwell Road, Kensington ☎ 020 7373 3300 🚇 Earl's Court

The Dorchester (£££)

World class; beautifully furnished bedrooms with sumptuous bathrooms, and everything you would expect at this level of service.
⊠ Park Lane ☎ 020 7629 8888 🚇 Hyde Park Corner

Foreign Missions Club (£)

With only gentle emphasis on the religious atmosphere, this converted row of terraced houses offers unexpected peace and quiet and a very friendly atmosphere, at exceptionally low cost.
⊠ 20–26 Aberdeen Park, Highbury ☎ 020 7226 2663 🚇 Highbury and Islington (10 minutes' walk)

London County Hall Travel Inn (££)

A large city-centre hotel that offers smart, spacious and well-equipped bedrooms, and is ideal for families.
⊠ Belvedere Road ☎ 0870 238 3300 🚇 Waterloo

Mitre House Hotel (££)

A long-established, family-run hotel with good facilities and all en-suite rooms, close to Hyde Park.
⊠ 178–184 Sussex Gardens ☎ 020 7723 8040 🚇 Lancaster Gate

Swiss House Hotel (££)

Comfortable, well-situated 16-room hotel in a pretty residential area of South Kensington, convenient for museums and shopping.
⊠ 171 Old Brompton Road, South Kensington ☎ 020 7373 2769 🚇 South Kensington, Gloucester Road

Thistle Tower (££)

A great location next to the Tower of London; large, busy and modern.
⊠ St Katharine's Way ☎ 020 7481 2575 🚇 Tower Hill

Northern England

Durham Marriott Hotel (££)
Set on the banks of the River Wear, the hotel, which has a good leisure centre and two styles of dining, is right in the heart of historic Durham, close to the cathedral and castle.

✉ **Old Elvet, Durham** ☎ **0191 386 6821**

Haleys Hotel & Restaurant (££)
An elegant Victorian town house hotel just over a mile from Leeds city centre, but in a quiet conservation area; boasts one of the best restaurants in Leeds.

✉ **Shire Oak Road, Headingley, Leeds** ☎ **0113 278 4446**

Le Meridien Victoria & Albert (££–£££)
Imaginatively created from old warehouses, this modern hotel stands on the banks of the River Irwell and provides easy access to Manchester's heritage and shopping sites; excellent restaurant.

✉ **Water Street, Manchester** ☎ **0161 832 1188**

Le Meridien York (££–£££)
Reminiscent of an age of past elegance, this magnificent, refurbished and restored Victorian hotel offers a pleasing atmosphere of romantic splendour and is set within its own private grounds overlooking the city walls.

✉ **Station Road, York** ☎ **01904 653681**

Miller Howe (££)
An established part of the Lakeland scene with an international reputation that is justly deserved; many bedrooms have private balconies overlooking Lake Windermere. Dinner is a unique experience that alone justifies staying here.

✉ **Rayrigg Road, Windermere, Cumbria** ☎ **015394 42536**

The Royal (££)
A listed Georgian building situated at Waterloo, just ten minutes by car from the city centre; the hotel looks out over Liverpool Bay, and the bedrooms are modern and well-equipped.

✉ **Marine Terrace, Waterloo, Liverpool** ☎ **0151 928 2332**

Shap Wells Hotel (££)
Cumbria's largest family-owned hotel, set in secluded, wooded ground mid-way between Kendal and Penrith, and only 5 minutes from junction 39 on the M6; ideal from which to explore the Lake District and Yorkshire Dales.

✉ **Shap, Penrith, Cumbria** ☎ **01931 716628**

Simonstone Hall Country House Hotel (££)
With lovely views over the Wensleydale countryside, this is a delightful base for exploring the Yorkshire Dales. The hotel is warm, friendly and has prettily decorated rooms with some antique furniture; interesting menus.

✉ **Simonstone, Hawes, North Yorkshire** ☎ **01969 667255**

Vermont Hotel (££–£££)
Friendly and stylish hotel next to the castle and conveniently located in the very heart of the buzzing quayside area.

✉ **Castle Garth, Newcastle upon Tyne** ☎ **0191 233 1010**

Booking a bed
If you arrive without having booked accommodation, don't worry. Contact the tourist information centre for the area in which you want to stay and you'll find them only too happy to make bookings for you for a small charge, which is deducted from your hotel bill. Once you get the hang of this system, you can use it to book your accommodation throughout your stay.

Central England

Chain Hotels

Throughout England there are several hotel chains all providing a similar standard of service and amenities, so that guests know exactly what to expect and what they will get for their money. Many chain hotels are on the edge of towns or close to major motorway junctions. They tend to be busy during the week and quieter at weekends when special rates can often be negotiated. Most offer a central reservation service: Best Western ☎ 0345 737373; Hilton ☎ 0845 7681595; Holiday Inn and Crown Plaza ☎ 0800 405060; Novotel ☎ 020 8283 4500; Thistle ☎ 0800 181716; Travel Inn ☎ 0870 2428000; Travelodge ☎ 0870 085 0950.

Bank House (£)

Originally a farmhouse, this delightful property has been lovingly restored. Bedrooms are well-equipped and guests dine family style with the owners.

✉ Farley Lane, Oakamoor, Staffordshire ☎ 01538 702810

Edgbaston Palace Hotel (££)

Built in 1854, the Edgbaston Palace Hotel is a Grade II listed building situated 1 mile (1.6km) from Birmingham city centre. All rooms offer a high standard of comfort and have en-suite facilities.

✉ 198 Hagley Road, Edgbaston, Birmingham ☎ 0121 452 1577

The Feathers at Ludlow (££)

This historic, long-established hotel dates back to the 17th century and features exposed timbers, ornate ceilings and oak panelling. The spacious and comfortable modern bedrooms are well-equipped.

✉ Bull Ring, Ludlow, Shropshire ☎ 01584 875261

Fownes Hotel (££)

The Victorian glove factory by the inner ring road has been converted into a successful, modern hotel with restaurant and well-furnished bedrooms.

✉ City Walls Road, Worcester ☎ 01905 613151

Le Manoir aux Quat' Saisons (£££)

It is the lovely gardens around this 15th-century manor house that supply the vegetables and herbs for the hotel's highly respected kitchens; an out-standing hotel and restaurant.

✉ Great Milton, Oxfordshire ☎ 01844 278881

Quorn Country Hotel (££)

A pleasant hotel with lovely landscaped grounds sweeping down to the River Soar. There are two restaurants offering different styles of cuisine and a generally friendly ambience.

✉ Charnwood House, Quorn, Leicestershire ☎ 01509 415050

Rutland Square Hotel (££)

An impressive conversion of a large red-brick warehouse, only 50yds (46m) from Nottingham Castle. The restaurant serves traditional English and French cuisine.

✉ St James Street, Nottingham ☎ 0115 941 1114

Tewkesbury Park Hotel & Country Club (££)

Set in 175 acres (71ha) of parkland on the southern edge of town, this hotel was built around an 18th-century mansion, and enjoys fine views over the River Severn. The bedrooms are all well-equipped, but the extensive leisure facilities are the main attraction.

✉ Lincoln Green Lane, Tewkesbury, Gloucestershire ☎ 0870 609 6101

Welcombe Hotel & Golf Course (£££)

Magnificent Jacobean-style mansion set in its own parkland with extensive formal gardens and 18-hole (par 70) golf course. Unrivalled views from a renowned restaurant, where French and regional cuisine are complemented by a fine, extensive wine cellar. Traditional afternoon teas and light snacks are served in an oak-panelled lounge.

✉ Warwick Road, Stratford-upon-Avon ☎ 01789 295252

Southwest England

The Ayrlington (££)
An elegant Victorian villa within a few minutes' walk of the Roman Baths and the city centre. The hotel, which overlooks the medieval abbey, offers an extensive range of facilities and quality accommodation.
✉ 24–25 Pulteney Road, Bath
☎ 01225 425495;
www.ayrlington .com

The Cornish Cottage Hotel & Restaurant (£–££)
Set amid the spectacular scenery of the north Cornish coast, the hotel has 14 rooms, all tastefully furnished and decorated; adjoining the hotel, the restaurant produces the very best of English and French cuisine.
✉ New Polzeath, near Rock, Cornwall ☎ 01208 862213

Hatton Court (££)
Set 600ft (183m) above sea level on top of Upton Hill, this manor house provides sweeping views across the River Severn to the Malvern Hills. The emphasis here is on comfort, and bedrooms are elegantly furnished.
✉ Upton Hill, Upton St Leonards, Gloucester ☎ 01452 617412

The Idle Rocks Hotel (£–££)
With commanding views over the quayside in St Mawes, this comfortable Cornish retreat is excellently placed for local walks and has a good restaurant.
✉ Harbourside, St Mawes, Cornwall ☎ 01326 270771

Manor House Hotel (££–£££)
Luxury in the heart of Dartmoor: elegant bedrooms, ornate public rooms, a fine restaurant, championship golf course and leisure facilities.
✉ Moretonhampstead, Devon
☎ 01647 440355

Stenhill Farm (£)
A bed and breakfast in a 500-year-old Devon longhouse, set in extensive grounds and farmland. Some bedrooms have four-poster beds.
✉ North Petherewin, Launceston, Cornwall
☎ 01566 785686; www.stenhill.com

Stock Hill Country House Hotel (£££)
The hotel, which also boasts an outstanding restaurant, stands in 11 acres (4.5ha) of parkland and is surrounded by rare old trees – a haven of peace and tranquillity. Charm and detailed elegance are the hallmark of all the rooms.
✉ Stock Hill, Gillingham, Dorset ☎ 01747 823626

The Thistle Bristol (££)
Though very centrally situated, this refurbished hotel offers quiet accommodation and all modern amenities; excellent secure car park. Also has an excellent health and leisure club.
✉ Broad Street, Bristol
☎ 0870 333 9130

White House Hotel (££)
Enjoy exploring the incomparable Quantocks from this most civilised haven, and then enjoy meals prepared with skill and imagination; winner of the César Award for combining French flair with English dependability.
✉ Long Street, Williton, Somerset ☎ 01984 632306

Hotel 'Charges' or 'Rates'
Most hotel rates are per person and inclusive of all taxes, service charges and breakfast, which usually means a full English breakfast, but do check this. Ironically, it is often the most expensive hotels that charge extra for breakfast.

Southeast England

B&Bs and Guest Houses

All across England there are literally thousands of, usually small, bed and breakfast places that offer basic, but friendly and welcoming, overnight accommodation, ideal for visitors who are constantly on the move. Slightly larger guest houses (which sometimes use the word 'hotel' in their name) generally provide a little more in terms of both service and amenities. These options are very much at the cheaper end of the scale, and usually give their prices on a per person basis, rather than for the room – be sure to check this. All the tourist information centres will help you with details of this kind of accommodation.

The Angel Posting House and Livery (£££)

A historic coaching inn in Guildford town centre, with exposed beams and Jacobean fireplaces. The restaurant serves modern British food but is in the characterful 13th-century crypt.

✉ **91 High Street, Guildford, Surrey** ☎ **01483 564555**

Beauport Park Hotel (££)

A Georgian country house hotel set in parkland with its own swimming pool, tennis courts, putting green, candle-lit restaurant and open log fires; close to 18- and 9-hole golf courses.

✉ **Hastings, East Sussex** ☎ **01424 851222**

Canterbury Hotel (££)

Not far from the cathedral and town centre, this is a family-run small, elegant hotel; bedrooms have pine furniture, and are well-equipped.

✉ **New Dover Road, Canterbury, Kent** ☎ **01227 450551**

Courtlands Hotel (££)

A long-established and popular hotel with a good range of bedrooms; all rooms are furnished in modern or traditional styles. Indoor heated pool.

✉ **15–27 The Drive, Hove, Brighton, East Sussex** ☎ **01273 731055**

Gravetye Manor (£££)

A stone-built Elizabethan mansion, the hotel stands at the end of a long drive through Forestry Commission land; the interior is characterised by highly polished wooden surfaces, open log fires, floral displays and spacious bedrooms with comfortable furniture and modern amenities.

✉ **East Grinstead, West Sussex** ☎ **01342 810567**

The Old Bridge Hotel (££)

The ultimate country hotel in a town. The lounges here extend into a really splendid conservatory where you can enjoy brasserie-style food or visit the top-class restaurant; all rooms are elegantly and comfortably furnished.

✉ **Huntingdon, Cambridgeshire** ☎ **01480 424300**

The Norfolk Mead Hotel (££)

Near Norwich and the Norfolk Broads, the hotel stands in secluded grounds by the River Bure, and has an excellent restaurant.

✉ **Church Loke, Coltishall, near Norwich, Norfolk** ☎ **01603 737531**

Ravenwood Hall Hotel (££)

Set in 7 acres of woodland and landscaped gardens just outside Bury St Edmunds, this is a hotel of character and quality; all the bedrooms are spaciously designed and thoughtfully equipped, and the welcoming restaurant provides a fixed-price menu. Outdoor heated pool.

✉ **Rougham, Bury St Edmunds, Suffolk** ☎ **01359 270345**

York House Hotel (££)

Situated in a spectacular sea-front setting, the hotel offers a high standard of accommodation, good food and wine, and a heated indoor swimming pool.

✉ **14–22 Royal Parade, Eastbourne, East Sussex** ☎ **01323 412918**

London Shopping Areas

Bond Street
London's most exclusive shopping street is expensive for buying, but a great place for just looking. *Haute couture*, antiques, auction houses, fine-art galleries and jewellers predominate.

🚇 **Green Park, Bond Street**

Charing Cross Road
A bookworm's heaven, for both new and used books. For general browsing try Blackwells, Book Etc, Foyles or Waterstones (➤ 104). For specialist, second-hand and antiquarian books, Cecil Court, off Charing Cross Road, is a gem.

🚇 **Leicester Square, Tottenham Court Road**

Covent Garden–Neal Street
Specialism is the key here with The Kite Store, The Hat Shop, The Bead Shop, and many other one-off stars. Neal's Yard attracts wholefood lovers, while young shoppers come for the high fashion on Short's Gardens.

🚇 **Covent Garden**

Covent Garden Piazza
Lots of small, individual, often idiosyncratic, shops in a buzzing traffic-free environment.

🚇 **Covent Garden**

Jermyn Street
Both a historical attraction and a shopping street, Jermyn Street is London shopping at its old-fashioned best.

🚇 **Green Park, Piccadilly Circus**

Kensington
Cheap and retro clothing can be found at Kensington Market, antiques and art abound on up-market Kensington Church Street, and behind the beautiful art deco front of Barkers is a good department store.

🚇 **High Street Kensington**

King's Road
Birthplace of the mini-skirt and the Punk movement, the King's Road is still up-to-the-minute on street fashion, but is less radical these days. This is also a good place to buy antiques and curios.

🚇 **Sloane Square**

Oxford Street
London's most frenetic shopping street presents a cacophony of global styles and noise and is good for chain stores and department stores. Off here at St Christopher's Place and South Molton Street (immediately north and south of Bond Street tube respectively) are some cutting-edge designer-fashion outlets.

🚇 **Marble Arch, Bond Street, Oxford Circus, Tottenham Court Rd**

Regent Street
A handsome boulevard with many exclusive shops including gold, silver and jewellery at Mappin & Webb and Garrard & Co; toys at Hamley's, and an emporium at Liberty.

🚇 **Oxford Circus, Piccadilly Circus**

Sloane Street
Chanel, Dior, Gucci, D&G, Hermès, Fendi, Boss, Prada, Roland Klein and Valentino are just some of the designer names to be found here.

🚇 **Sloane Square (south end), Knightsbridge (north end)**

Shop Opening Times
Traditionally London shop opening hours have been Monday to Saturday 9:30–6. Many West End stores, including Oxford and Regent streets, stay open later on Thursdays; in Knightsbridge late night is Wednesdays. More recently, however, several shops are opening later at other times and also on Sunday (from 11 or noon). If opening times are not indicated in the entry then you can assume that they operate more-or-less traditional hours. In tourist enclaves such as Covent Garden, Sunday opening is the norm.

Antiques, Books and Collectables

Shopping

Napoleon once described the British as 'a nation of shopkeepers', and, as in modern times, shopping is a major leisuretime pursuit. The development of massive, out-of-town shopping complexes has only fuelled the debate about whether they are killing off the town centre shopping areas in the same way that many of the small village shops, which were a common feature of the rural scene, have been closed down by competition from the towns.

Antiques

England has a host of antique shops, though they range from little more than glorified junk shops to highly priced antique businesses selling only the finest items. If money is no object, then you could try attending one of the numerous auctions held (usually) in London at Sotheby's, for example, but there are auctions held throughout the country and you have only to read local newspapers to discover when and where.

But, if it's the thrill of discovering something unusual, valuable or rare, or just the inexplicable pleasure that comes from browsing you enjoy, you should look out for notices announcing car boot sales. This odd phenomenon of current English marketing is, if we're being honest, simply a means of clearing out attics and cellars, and getting rid of unwanted items, while earning a little in the process. Among the items on offer, however, you can always find something of interest and quite often items of value, too – don't forget, most of the people who are doing the selling have no idea of the real value of antiques, and as a result you can pick up items at ridiculously low prices. Most towns and many villages hold regular car boot sales, which have to be licensed, and so relatively reliable.

You should also keep an eye open for news of antique fairs. Most people selling at these are professionals and know the value of what they're selling, so you are less likely to get a bargain, but more likely to get a good-value item.

Books

If you want second-hand books, then *the* place to go is Hay-on-Wye. Hay is, strictly speaking, just in Wales, but part of this small town is also just inside Herefordshire, in England, and so can be included in this guide. The whole town seems to be a series of second-hand bookshops, and if you can't find the book you're looking for here, you probably won't find it anywhere. Of course, most towns have second-hand book dealers, but the knack of shopping for second-hand books is not to buy a book in its own locality – local people know the real value of books. Books about the Yorkshire Dales, for example, are best bought along the south coast, a book on the West Country may be easier to find in faraway Carlisle than Bath or Wells. For new books, the main book store 'chains' are Waterstone's, County Books, WH Smith, Borders and Ottakers.

Collectables

Up and down the country there are regular 'fairs' selling collectable items such as postage stamps, toys, bric-a-brac, clothes and military costumes. These are often held in old town hall buildings, the antiquated surroundings seeming well-suited to this form of selling. As 'fairs' they bear little resemblance to the traditional country fairs of old (▶ 105), but can be great fun.

Markets, Department Stores, Other Shops

Markets

You'll find markets in almost every town in England. Many towns have long-established rights to hold markets that were granted by past kings and queens, in some cases as long ago as the 12th century. These market rights are still in existence, jealously protected and often commemorated each year, as, for example, in Kendal and Broughton-in-Furness. Markets sell a wide range of goods and food products, from fresh fish and meat to clothing and haberdashery, always at competitive prices, making them an ideal place to buy essential items. London has some fine street markets – on Brick Lane in the East End, the Borough and Camden to name but a few. Elsewhere you will find some towns and cities, such as Sheffield, Birmingham and Leeds, have permanent covered market halls, where others have large outside areas with temporary stalls. It is often the less glamourous towns, such as Barnsley, Long Eaton or Moreton-in-Marsh, which have the best markets.

Department Stores

The most famous and popular of the big department stores are in London, for example Harrods (▶ 106), Harvey Nichols, Selfridges and Fortnum & Mason (▶ 106), but there are national chain stores represented in every town. These include long-established businesses like Marks & Spencer, Woolworths, Laura Ashley, British Home Stores (BHS), and Littlewoods.

Shopping Complexes

Many large towns now have massive, mall-style shopping precincts, some in the centre, for example, Arndale in Manchester or the Harlequin in Watford. Others are out of town; Gateshead's Metro Centre, Thurrock's Lakeside or Sheffield's Meadowhall. The vast size of the developments has changed the face of many towns and you will often find that the entire local transport system has shifted its emphasis towards servicing the malls.

Charity Shops

You'll find charity shops in every shopping area in every town. Taking advantage of favourable business rates, they sell everything from books to household goods and clothing to raise money for charity. The main charity shops are Oxfam, Barnardo's, British Heart Foundation, Cancer Research and Help the Aged, and they are usually run by volunteers.

Fairs

Traditionally, fairs may only be held once or twice a year. Although similar in their commercial origin to markets, they largely concentrated on the sale of livestock at the end of the year. When the harvest was finished, farmhands needed to look for work, and a tradition grew up of hiring fairs, at which employers and employees could meet. Today the retail element has almost entirely slipped away and most fairs around the country are funfairs with rides, candyfloss and fast-food stalls.

Market Crosses
Many of the traditional market towns throughout England still have a market cross as their focal point. The earliest market charters were granted by the king during the 13th and 14th centuries. They conferred the right to hold weekly markets selling a variety of produce. The market cross was erected to identify the market's centre. In some towns, they have been adapted to become war memorials or monuments to local dignitaries.

Food & Drink

By Royal Appointment
Many shops throughout England, but mainly in London and the formerly important or 'royal' towns, claim a Royal Warrant of Appointment. These can only be granted by the Queen, the Queen Mother, the Prince of Wales and the Duke of Edinburgh, and signify that one of these members of the royal family has patronised the shop for at least three years. The coat (or coats) of arms on display outside the shop indicates which member.

Supermarkets

If you simply want to buy foodstuffs while 'on the move', there is a number of large supermarkets that have developed across the whole of England; they sell a wide and comprehensive range of food and drinks, and often sell clothing, hardware, household goods, books, magazines, car repair items, too – in fact, just about everything you're ever likely to need. The main supermarket chains are Sainsbury, Tesco, Asda, Safeway, Waitrose, Somerfield and Morrisons. There are also very cheap European chainstores and a number of regional supermarket groups.

Specialist Shops

Away from the supermarkets, the best food can only be found in specialist shops and here are a few examples.

London

Fortnum & Mason
World famous for supplying the most fabulous hampers.
⊠ **181 Piccadilly** ☎ **020 7734 8040**

Harrods
This huge department store has one of the finest food halls in the land and 330 different departments..
⊠ **87–135 Brompton Road, Knightsbridge** ☎ **0207730 1234**

Paxton & Whitfield
Cheese specialists where you can even order a cheese to be ripe on a particular day.
⊠ **93 Jermyn Street** ☎ **020 7930 0259**

Northern England
J&J Graham
Traditional town-centre delicatessen and grocer.
⊠ **Market Square, Penrith, Cumbria** ☎ **01768 862281**

Betty's of Harrogate
Buy the finest loose tea, or relax in their famous tea rooms (▶ 94)
⊠ **1 Parliament Street, Harrogate, N Yorks** ☎ **01423 502746**

Central England
Dickinson and Morris
A veritable shrine to the excellent pork pies, still produced on the premises in the traditional way.
⊠ **8–10 Nottingham Street, Melton Mowbray, Leicestershire** ☎ **01664 562341**

Southwest England
Burrow Hill Cider
Traditionally made cider from local apples.
⊠ **Pass Vale Farm, Burrow Hill, Kingsbury Episcopi, Somerset** ☎ **01460 240782**

Cheddar Gorge Cheese Company
Watch a variety of different cheeses being made.
⊠ **The Cliffs, Cheddar Gorge, Somersert** ☎ **01934 742810**

Southeast England
Coleman's Mustard Shop
Norwich is synonymous with mustard, made from England's only native spice.
⊠ **15 Royal Arcade, Norwich, Norfolk** ☎ **01603 627889**

Lurgashall Winery
Fruit wines and other food and drink made using local ingredients using traditional techniques.
⊠ **Dial Green, Lurgashall, near Petworth** ☎ **01428 707292**

London

Covent Garden
The pedestrianised area here always seems to have free outdoor entertainment. There are loads of different places to eat, and the London Transport Museum makes a fascinating visit.

London Zoo
Opened in 1827 and home to more than 12,000 animals, insects, reptiles and fish, including rare and exotic species.
✉ Regent's Park ☎ 020 7722 3333 🕐 Summer 10–5:30; winter 10–4 Ⓜ Camden Town 💷 Expensive

Madame Tussaud's
World leaders, murderers, sportsmen and film actors stand side by side in this legendary exhibition of wax figures.
✉ Marylebone Road ☎ 0870 400 3000 🕐 Mon–Fri 10–5:30, Sat–Sun 9:30–5:30; Easter and Jun–Aug, daily 9–5:30 Ⓜ Baker Street 💷 Very expensive

Messing About on Boats
Exploring the decks and cramped living quarters of historic boats and warships is always fascinating, and London has a good number of them, some moored on the Thames, others in dry dock. At Greenwich the *Cutty Sark* stands tall above Francis Chichester's diminutive *Gipsy Moth IV*. Elsewhere you can explore HMS *Belfast* and the *Golden Hind*, a replica of Sir Francis Drake's flagship. Or you can simply enjoy a boat trip on the Thames from Westminster Pier (by Westminster Bridge).
Ⓜ Westminster

National Maritime Museum
Britain's seafaring history; the world of Nelson and the glory of the British Empire; 20th-century seapower and luxury liners.
✉ Romney Road, Greenwich ☎ 020 8858 4422 🕐 Daily 10–5 🚉 DLR: Cutty Sark 💷 Free

Pollock's Toy Museum
One of London's most fascinating museums, crammed full of historic toys, games and miniature theatres; of great interest to children of all ages.
✉ 41 Whitfield Street ☎ 020 7636 3452 🕐 Mon–Sat 10–5 Ⓜ Goodge Street 💷 Cheap

Smollensky's on the Strand
Weekend lunchtimes are best, when the special children's entertainment includes clowns, magicians, face painting and Nintendo games.
✉ 105 Strand ☎ 020 7497 2101 Ⓜ Embankment, Charing Cross

Tower of London
Always a favourite with children, especially the Beefeaters with their tales of executions and gruesome exploits (➤ 24).

Trocadero
A massive, multi-level complex of techno-thrills with white-knuckle rides, video games, hi-tech exhibitions, virtual reality adventures, state-of-the-art motion simulators, cinema, restaurant and shops.
✉ Coventry Street, Piccadilly ☎ 0906 888 1100 🕐 Sun–Thu 10am–midnight, Fri–Sat 10AM–1AM Ⓜ Piccadilly Circus 💷 Expensive

Kid's Out
Keep an eye open for *Kid's Out*, the name of an excellent monthly 'what's-on-for-children' magazine published by *Time Out*. There is a special website (www.kidslovelondon. com), which is for children to surf.

107

Northern England

There's So Much More

The listings given in these pages are just a small selection from a vast range. All the local tourist information centres will have details of many more facilities, some of which have discounted promotions and entry charges for people who can visit at off-peak times; it's always worth checking out.

Aquarium of the Lakes

Follow a river from mountain top to sea, and meet Britain's largest collection of freshwater fish.

✉ Lakeside, Newby Bridge, Cumbria ☎ 015395 30153; www.aquariumofthelakes.co.uk ⏰ Daily summer 9–5; winter 9–4 ♿ Moderate

Blackpool Sea Life Centre

Take a walk through the underwater tunnel and be surrounded by some of the oceans' greatest predators.

✉ The Promenade, Blackpool ☎ 01253 622445 ⏰ Summer 10–9; winter 10–5 (times vary, telephone to confirm) ♿ Moderate

Camelot Theme Park & Rare Breeds Farm

Daily jousting tournaments, indoor entertainment centre and interactive facilities.

✉ Park Hall Road, Charnock Richard, Chorley, Lancashire ☎ 01257 453044, 01257 452100 (24-hour information line); www.camelotthemepark.co.uk ⏰ late Mar–Oct, daily 10–5 ♿ Expensive

Chester Zoo

One of Europe's finest zoological gardens with 6,000 animals in 110 acres (44ha).

✉ Upton-by-Chester, Chester ☎ 01244 380280; www.chesterzoo.org.uk ⏰ Daily 10–4:30/7 depending on season ♿ Expensive

Earth Centre

Built to commemorate the millennium and set in 350 acres (142ha), comprising four main areas: Planet Earth; Water Works; a children's theatre; and a nature centre.

✉ Denaby Main, Doncaster ☎ 01709 512000 ⏰ Apr–Nov, daily 10–6 ♿ Expensive

Eureka

Award-winning hands-on museum of science designed especially for children.

✉ Discovery Road, Halifax, W Yorks ☎ 01422 330069, 07626 983191 (recorded information); www.eureka.org.uk ⏰ Daily 10–5 except 24–26 Dec ♿ Moderate

Magna

Science adventure centre exploring earth, air, fire, water and power with lots of hands-on, interactive challenge. There are five adventure pavilions, two shows and an outdoor adventure park.

✉ Sheffield Road, Templeborough, Rotherham ☎ 01709 720002; www.magnatrust.org.uk ⏰ Daily 10–5; closed 24–25 Dec ♿ Moderate

New Metroland

Europe's largest indoor funfair theme park. Have fun in Monty Zoomer's children's adventure area and see the talking clocks.

✉ 39 Garden Walk, Gateshead MetroCentre ☎ 0191 493 2048; www.metroland.uk.com ⏰ Mon–Fri 12–8 (10–8 during school holidays), Sat 9–8, Sun 11–7 ♿ Moderate

Sellafield Visitors Centre

Hands-on interactive scientific experiments at the country's foremost nuclear power plant. Not everyone's ideal attraction, but nevertheless an absorbing exhibition for a wet day in the Lake District.

✉ Sellafield, Seascale, Cumbria ⏰ Daily Apr–Sep 10–5; Oct–Mar 10–4 ♿ Free

Central England

Alton Towers
The white-knuckle rides at Alton Towers make it the scream capital of Britain; here the techno-dammed can be twisted and corkscrewed to their heart's (or stomach's) content.

✉ Alton, Staffordshire
☎ 0870 444 4455; www.alton-towers.co.uk 🕐 Apr–Oct, daily 9:30–5/6:30 depending on season 💷 Expensive

Drayton Manor Theme Park and Zoo
The park has over 100 rides including Shockwave and Fifth Element and a zoo with animals from reptiles to big cats.

✉ Near Tamworth, Staffordshire ☎ 01827 287979
🕐 Mar–Nov, daily 10:30–5/7
💷 Expensive

Gulliver's Kingdom
Lots of rides, including wild west street and alpine log flume.

✉ Temple Walk, Matlock Bath, Derbyshire ☎ 01629 580540; www.gulliversfun.co.uk
🕐 Late Mar–Oct, daily 10:30–5
💷 Moderate

Ironbridge Gorge Museums
The world's first iron bridge was cast and built here in 1779. Now the site of a splendid series of ten historical industrial museums and exhibitions that are endlessly fascinating (➤ 59).

✉ Ironbridge, Telford, Shropshire ☎ 01952 432166 or 433522 🕐 Daily 10–5. Some museums closed Nov–Mar
💷 Moderate–expensive; ask about a passport to all museums

National Sea Life Centre
Britain's first inland sea life development, boasting a completely transparent underwater tunnel and a *Titanic* exhibition.

✉ The Waters Edge, Brindley Place, Birmingham ☎ 0121 643 6777 🕐 Daily 10–5
💷 Moderate

National Waterways Museum
Award-winning museum with working models and engines, archive film, hands-on exhibits and interactive displays.

✉ Llanthony Warehouse, Gloucester Docks, Gloucester
☎ 01452 318200; www.nwm.org.uk 🕐 Daily 10–5
💷 Moderate

Santa Pod Raceway
The home of European drag racing, attracting over 200,000 visitors each season.

✉ Airfield Road, Podington, Wellingborough, Northamptonshire ☎ 01234 782828 🕐 Mar–Nov, most weekends, times vary
💷 Expensive; buy a day ticket

Speedwell Cavern
Go down 105 steps to a boat that takes you more than a mile through underground, water-filled caverns.

✉ Winnats Pass, Castleton, Derbyshire ☎ 01433 620512; www.speedwellcavern.co.uk
🕐 Daily 9:30–4:30
💷 Moderate

Waterworld
Home of the UK's first indoor roller coaster, plus 16 other water attractions housed in a constant tropical atmosphere.

✉ Festival Park, Festival Way, Etruria, Staffordshire ☎ 01782 205747 🕐 Sat–Tue and BH 10–6, Wed 10–7, Thu 10–8, Fri 10–9 💷 Moderate

Discount Tickets
Throughout the year it is quite commonplace for the national, regional and local newspapers to run special promotions that enable readers to obtain admission charge discount tickets that operate at most of the participating attractions. Cast an occasional eye over the news-stands for special offers that coincide with your visit.

Southwest England

Hours of Opening

Many of the attractions and facilities listed in these pages have variable opening hours, some changing almost daily according to demand. It is always wise to phone first to check the times of opening on the day of your visit, to avoid disappointment or a wasted journey.

Cotswold Wildlife Park

In the landscaped park around a Gothic-style manor house is a varied collection of animals from ants to rhinos, plus a sizeable reptile collection, an aquarium and children's farmyard.

🖂 **Bradwell Grove, Burford, Oxfordshire** ☎ **01993 823006** 🕓 **Daily Mar–Sep 10–5 (4 or dusk in winter)** 💷 **Moderate**

Flambards Village

Family attraction including Victorian village, rides, Aviation display, Science Centre and wartime displays.

🖂 **Culdrose Manor, Helston, Cornwall** ☎ **01326 573404** 🕓 **Apr to mid-Jul, Sep–Oct 10–5; mid-Jul to Aug 10:30–6 (times and dates vary, phone to check)** 💷 **Expensive; but includes all rides and entertainment**

Isle of Wight Steam Railway

Steam trains run the five miles from Wootton, via Havenstreet to Smallbrook Junction.

🖂 **Station Road, Havenstreet Village, Ryde** ☎ **01983 882204** 🕓 **Late May–late Sep, daily 10–4:30, plus some days in Mar, Apr, Oct and Dec (phone for times)** 💷 **Moderate**

Living Rainforest

A conservation project housed in three rainforest climates under 20,000sq ft (1,860sq m) of glass.

🖂 **Hampstead Norreys, Thatcham, Berkshire** ☎ **01635 202444** 🕓 **Daily 10–5:15** 💷 **Cheap–moderate**

Longleat

This renowned safari park with lions, wolves, giraffes, gorillas and zebras is sure to produce an exciting time for everyone (▶ 75).

🖂 **Warminster, Wiltshire** ☎ **01985 844400** 🕓 **Apr–Oct, daily 10–5 (dusk if earlier)** 💷 **Expensive**

National Marine Aquarium

A state-of-the-art development, including Europe's largest collection of seahorses; there are also touch pools, and a large tank containing sharks.

🖂 **Rope Walk, Coxside, Plymouth** ☎ **01752 600301; www.nationalaquarium.co.uk** 🕓 **Apr–Oct, daily 10–5; Nov–Mar, daily 10–5** 💷 **Moderate**

National Seal Sanctuary

Britain's largest marine rescue centre, accommo-dating more than 30 seal pups annually, which are rehabilitated and then released.

🖂 **Gweek, Cornwall** ☎ **01326 221361** 🕓 **Daily 9–5:30 (4:30 in winter)** 💷 **Moderate**

Tropiquaria

Housed in a 1930s radio transmitter station, Tropiquaria is an indoor jungle with an aquarium, tropical plants and parrots.

🖂 **Washford Cross, Watchet, Somerset** ☎ **01984 640688; www.tropiquaria.co.uk** 🕓 **Late Mar to mid-Sep, daily, 10–5; mid-Sep to Oct, daily, 11–4; Nov–Easter, Sat–Sun 11–4 (28 Dec–5 Jan daily)** 💷 **Cheap–moderate**

Woodlands Leisure Park

Park with lots of indoor and outdoor attractions, including 15 play zones, falconry centre and other animals.

🖂 **Blackawton, Totnes, Devon** ☎ **01803 712598** 🕓 **Mid-Mar to mid-Nov, daily 9:30–dusk; mid-Nov to mid-Mar, Sat, Sun and school hols from 9** 💷 **Moderate**

Southeast England

Beale Park
Rare and endangered birds, plus a narrow-gauge railway and model boat collection.
✉ **Lower Basildon, Berkshire** ☎ **0118 984 5172** ⏱ **Mar–late Dec, daily 10–6** 💷 **Moderate**

Buckinghamshire Railway Centre
A working steam museum with full-size and miniature railways; over 35 locomotives.
✉ **Quainton Road Station, Quainton, Buckinghamshire** ☎ **01296 655720** ⏱ **Steam days: Apr–Oct, Sun and BH 10–6, also Jul–Aug, Wed 11–5. Static viewing days: Apr–Oct, Sat 11–4; Jan–Mar and Nov, Sun 11–4** 💷 **Cheap–moderate**

Butterfly and Wildlife Park
One of Britain's largest walk-through butterfly houses with exotic butterflies, Reptile Land, an insectarium, adventure playground, pets corner and picnic areas.
✉ **Long Sutton, Lincolnshire** ☎ **01406 363833** ⏱ **Apr–Oct, daily 10–5** 💷 **Moderate**

Chessington World of Aventures
Theme park with exciting white-knuckle rides like the 'Vampire' rollercoaster.
✉ **Chessington, Surrey** ☎ **0870 444 7777; www. chessington.co.uk** ⏱ **Apr–Oct 10–(closing times vary)** 💷 **Expensive**

Howletts Wild Animal Park
Boasting the world's largest breeding gorilla colony in captivity and Britain's most successful herd of breeding African elephants.
✉ **Bekesbourne, Canterbury, Kent** ☎ **09068 800605** ⏱ **Daily 10–5 (3:30 in winter)** 💷 **Expensive**

Legoland Windsor
This gloriously landscaped theme park in miniature is dedicated to the imagination and creativity of children. It was specifically designed for the under-12s and will easily keep kids amused for a day.
✉ **Windsor Park, Windsor, Berkshire** ☎ **0870 504 0404; www.legoland.co.uk** ⏱ **Daily 10–6 (mid-Jul to early Sep 10–8)** 💷 **Very expensive**

Norfolk Broads Wildlife Centre & Country Park
A large collection of British and European wildlife set in parkland, with a pets corner, play areas, model farm and trout pool.
✉ **Great Witchingham, Norfolk** ☎ **01603 872274; www. norfolkwildlife.co.uk** ⏱ **Apr–Oct, daily 10–5** 💷 **Moderate**

Paradise Park
A unique attraction with an undercover botanical garden incorporating a cacti house and rainforest; gardens with lakes, Sussex in Miniature, small-gauge railway. Planet Earth and the Living Dinosaur Museum have interactive displays and many rare fossils.
✉ **Avis Road, Newhaven, East Sussex** ☎ **01273 512123; recorded information 616006** ⏱ **Daily 9–6** 💷 **Moderate**

Thorpe Park
All the thrills, spills and excitement of the UK's wettest theme park.
✉ **Staines Road, Chertsey, Surrey** ☎ **0870 444 4466; www.thorpepark.co.uk** ⏱ **Late Mar to mid-Sep and end Oct, daily 9:30/10–5/5:30; mid-Sep to late Oct, Thu–Mon 9:30/10–5/5:30 (phone for details)** 💷 **Expensive**

Theme Parks
Before you head for one of England's excellent theme parks, check out the access restrictions for the major rides. Many have age and height rules which could spoil a day if you only discovered them on arrival. You can also make enquiries about the length of time people usually spend in the queues for the top attractions and what provisions are made for younger children or visitors with disabilities.

Arts and Culture

The West End

Many of the West End theatres feature world-renowned long-running musicals (*Miss Saigon, Cats, Les Misérables, Phantom of the Opera* and so on), others stage modern plays and short-run musical performances. Tickets for London shows can be expensive and hard to come by. The box office should be your first port of call, but you can also try legitimate ticket agents like Ticketmaster (☎ 0870 534 4444; www. ticketmaster.co.uk) or First Call (☎ 0870 906 3838; www.firstcalltickets.com), who may be able to help. Don't use ticket touts.

The Society of London Theatres' (SOLT) half-price ticket booth sells tickets for that day's performances, though they are generally top-of-the-range seats and unlikely to be for the major performances.
✉ **Leicester Square** ⏲ **Mon–Sat, 10–7, Sun, 12–3:30 for matinées only** 💳 **Cash, credit and debit cards (or theatre tokens) only. Service charge £2.50 per ticket** Ⓜ **Leicester Square, Piccadilly Circus**

London

London boasts many long-running shows, mainly in the West End, as well as mainstream theatres presenting Shakespeare and contemporary playwrights.

Barbican Centre

Europe's largest arts centre is the base for the London Symphony and English Chamber orchestras. Formerly the London home of the Royal Shakespeare Company, it still stages some RSC performances, and has art galleries and cinemas.
✉ **Silk Street, EC2** ☎ **020 7628 2326** Ⓜ **Barbican/Moorgate**

Royal Opera House

The Covent Garden home of the Royal Ballet and the Royal Opera. Free lunchtime concerts and events in the new Linbury Studio Theatre.
✉ **Bow Street, Covent Garden** ☎ **020 7304 4000** Ⓜ **Covent Garden, Embankment**

Sadler's Wells Theatre

Sadler's Wells is the centre of British contemporary dance as well as hosting touring companies.
✉ **Rosebery Avenue** ☎ **020 7863 8000; www. sadlerswells.com** Ⓜ **Angel**

South Bank Centre

In a boldly modernist building on the South Bank of the Thames, the centre hosts top-class contemporary European dance groups. The English National Ballet gives annual performances of *The Nutcracker* in January, then returns for a summer season.
✉ **South Bank** ☎ **020 7960 4242** Ⓜ **Waterloo**

Northern England

Bridgewater Hall

Recitals by the Hallé Orchestra and the BBC Philharmonic, plus one-off shows.
✉ **Lower Mosley Street, Manchester** ☎ **0161 907 9000**

Everyman Theatre

From Shakespeare to stand-up comedy.
✉ **1 Hope Street, Liverpool** ☎ **0151 709 4776**

Grand Theatre and Opera House

Opera North and full range of theatrical productions.
✉ **Briggate, Leeds** ☎ **0113 222 6222**

Lyceum Theatre

Drama, touring shows, ballet, opera.
✉ **55 Norfolk Street, Sheffield** ☎ **0114 249 6000**

Philharmonic Hall

Concerts by the world-renowned Royal Liverpool Philharmonic orchestra.
✉ **Hope Street, Liverpool** ☎ **0151 709 3789**

The Playhouse

Modern theatre and performances by the Northern Stage Company.
✉ **Barras Bridge, Newcastle** ☎ **0191 230 5151**

Theatre Royal

✉ **100 Grey Street, Newcastle** ☎ **0870 905 5060**

Central England

Birmingham Repertory Theatre

Two theatres since 1913; the main house (seats 900) and Studio Theatre (140).
✉ **Broad Street, Birmingham** ☎ **0121 2452000**

Holywell Music Room
Everything from classical to experimental music, jazz, plays and opera.
✉ 32 Holywell Street, Oxford
☎ 01865 305305

Hippodrome Theatre
The home of Birmingham Royal Ballet as well as regularly hosting the Welsh National Opera.
✉ Hurst Street, Birmingham
☎ 0870 7305555

Midland Arts Centre
Well supported by touring theatre companies.
✉ Cannon Hill Park, Edgbaston, Birmingham ☎ 0121 440 3838

Pegasus Theatre
For avant garde productions.
✉ Magdalen Road, Oxford
☎ 01865 722851

Playhouse
With the Holywell Music Room, provides the bulk of music and theatre in Oxford.
✉ Beaumont Street, Oxford
☎ 01865 305305;
www.oxfordplayhouse.com

Stratford-upon-Avon Theatres
For all things Shakespearean, the Royal Shakespeare Theatre; for works contemporary with Shakespeare, The Swan; and for modern and experimental works, The Other Place in Southern Lane.
☎ 0870 6091110 box office; 01789 403405 tours

Symphony Hall
Birmingham boasts the acclaimed City of Birmingham Symphony Orchestra, which performs at the acoustically magnificent Symphony Hall,

the venue also for a host of touring music and opera recitals.
✉ International Convention Centre, Centenary Square, Birmingham ☎ 0121 780 3333

Southwest and Southeast England
Arts Theatre
Cambridge's main theatre, which launched the careers of actors such as Stephen Fry and Derek Jacobi, provides an eclectic range of productions.
✉ Park Street, Cambridge
☎ 01223 503333

Axiom Centre for the Arts
Features a wide range of non-mainstream music and theatre.
✉ 57 Winchcombe Street, Cheltenham ☎ 01242 253183

Chichester Festival Theatre
Classic and contemporary theatre.
✉ Oaklands Park, Chichester
☎ 01243 781312; www.cft.org.uk

Colston Hall
Bristol's main venue, promoting major names in classical and popular music and its own classical Proms.
✉ Colston Street, Bristol
☎ 0117 922 3686

Everyman Theatre
Produces many shows from Shakespeare to stand-up comedy.
✉ Regent Street, Cheltenham
☎ 01242 572573

Theatre Royal, Bath
Drama and ballet are regularly featured at the Theatre Royal, which also has a separate studio for experimental works.
✉ Sawclose ☎ 01225 448844;
www.theatreroyal.org.uk

Festivals
The arts festival is a popular way for a town to raise its profile and generate income for its venues and accommodation. Some are tiny and little more than marketing wheezes, others are major international events, hosting top-of-the-range performers. For classical music the festivals at Aldburgh in Suffolk (☎ 01728 687100), Buxton in Derbyshire (☎ 01298 70395) and Cheltenham in Gloucestershire (☎ 01242 227979) are particular highlights.

Sport, Live Music and Comedy

Classical Music Recitals

Each year the major London and provincial orchestras present a series of 'Proms' (promenade concerts), originally founded by Henry Wood in London. The emphasis is on light-hearted musical entertainment, but without compromising the quality of the music. Traditionally, the 'Last Night of the Proms' is quite special, with patriotic songs and flag waving. Tickets go early and quickly.

Popular Music and Jazz

A wide range of of styles makes up the English music scene, from jazz and folk through to soul, R&B and mainstream pop and rock. Among the interesting venues around the country are:

London

The 100 Club
✉ **100 Oxford Street**
☎ **020 7636 0933**
Ⓜ **Oxford Circus**

Barfly
✉ **49 Chalk Farm Road**
☎ **020 7791 4246;**
www.barflyclub.com
Ⓜ **Oxford Circus**

Brixton Academy
✉ **Stockwell Road, Brixton**
☎ **020 7771 3000**

The Jazz Café
✉ **5 Parkway, Camden Town**
☎ **020 7916 6060**
Ⓜ **Camden Town**

Ronnie Scott's
✉ **47 Frith Street**
☎ **020 7439 0747**
Ⓜ **Leicester Square**

Royal Albert Hall
✉ **Kensington Gore, Knightsbridge** ☎ **020 7589 8212**
Ⓜ **South Kensington**

Wembley Arena
☎ **0870 739 0739**
Ⓜ **Wembley Park**

Northern England
Band on the Wall
The best in jazz, blues, folk and pop.
✉ **Swan Street, Manchester**
☎ **0161 832 6625**

Bluecoats Arts Centre
Eclectic mix of drama, dance, music and art.
✉ **School Lane, Liverpool**
☎ **0151 709 5297**

Bridge Hotel
Folk, blues and jazz, plus Tyneside Blues Festival every April.
✉ **Castle Square, St Nicholas St, Newcastle** ☎ **0191 232 6400**

Jongleurs Leeds
Comedy Club (Friday and Saturday night only) in a complex including two dance floors and several bars.
✉ **'The Cube', Albion Street, Leeds** ☎ **0870 7870707**

The Manchester Evening News Arena
20,000-seater indoor concert stadium.
✉ **Victoria Station, Hunts Bank, Manchester**
☎ **0870 190 8000**

Royal Northern College of Music
Quality modern jazz concerts.
✉ **124 Oxford Road, Manchester**
☎ **0161 907 5200**

Central England
Jongleurs Birmingham
Huge comedy club seating 2,400 on two floors with bars, dance area and lounge.
✉ **Broad Street, Birmingham**
☎ **0870 7870707**

National Exhibition Centre (NEC)
✉ **Birmingham,** ☎ **0870 9094133**

Theatre Royal and Royal Concert Hall
Nottingham's top venue for plays, musicals, comedy, opera and classical concerts.
✉ **Theatre Square, Nottingham**
☎ **0115 9895500**

Southwest and Southeast England

Bournemouth International Centre
Three venues in one at popular resort town.
✉ **Exeter Road, Bournemouth**
☎ **01202 456456**

Fleece and Firkin
Loud and sweaty; live music and comedy.
✉ **12 St Thomas Street, Bristol**
☎ **0117 945 0996**

Glastonbury
Renowned for its (mainly) pop music festival at the end of June in nearby Pilton, the biggest and best in the country, with big-name bands to up-and-coming groups.
☎ **01749 890470**

The Jazz Place
Popular jazz venue.
✉ **Smugglers Inn, 10 Ship Street, Brighton** ☎ **01273 328439**

Komedia
Alternative theatre and stand-up comedy.
✉ **14-17 Manchester Street, Brighton**

New Trinity Centre
Good small venue.
✉ **Trinity Road, off Old Market, Bristol** ☎ **0117 907 7119**

Norwich Arts Centre
One of East Anglia's top venues for the performing arts, including major touring pop and rock bands.
✉ **Reeves Yard, off St Benedict's Street, Norwich**
☎ **01603 660352**

Star and Garter
Bristol's best reggae venue.
✉ **33 Brook Road, Montpelier, Bristol** ☎ **0117 940 5552**

Sport
Cricket
Although cricket originated in England, the national team has slumped to the bottom of the international rankings in this absorbing though often bewildering sport. Test matches with international opposition are played around the country, notably at Lord's in London (☎ **020 7432 1066**), Edgbaston in Birmingham (☎ **0121 446 5506**) and Old Trafford) in Manchester (☎ **0161 282 4040**)

Football (Soccer)
Manchester United (☎ **0161 8688631**) is one of the world's most sucessful football clubs, but tickets to home games are very hard to come by. Liverpool and Leeds United challenge their domination in the north, whilst Arsenal and Chelsea are London's most successful teams. You'll find smaller clubs all over England. For details of Premier League matches call ☎ **020 7298 1600.**

Horse Racing
There are racecourses all over England, with betting licensed on and off the course. For more information look at the British Horseracing Board website. **www.bhb.co.uk**.

Rugby
Twickenham, near London, is the National Stadium and headquarters of the Rugby Football Union (☎ **020 8892 2000**). Rugby League is played mostly in Northern England where Leeds, Bradford, Wigan and St Helens are the big clubs. (National Office ☎ **0113 232 9111**).

Agricultural Shows
Many of the rural villages throughout the length and breadth of England have summertime agricultural shows that contain displays of rural crafts and skills, sheepdog trials, farm breeds competitions and local sports; without exception they are wonderfully entertaining experiences for all the family.

What's On When

What's On

These listings contain only a selection, generally the more famous, of England's entertainment options (some with a touch of eccentricity). For up-to-date information on what is available throughout the regions, it is essential to consult the regional tourist boards (► 120). For arts, literature and music festival information (► 113) try www.artsfestivals.co.uk or www.festivals.demon.co.uk. for more information.

January
Lord Mayor's Parade, London

February
Chinese New Year celebrations in Liverpool, Manchester and London

March
Irish Festival, Manchester
Crufts Dog Show, NEC, Birmingham
University Boat Race, London

April
Oxford and Cambridge Boat Race, River Thames, London
Padstow Fish and Ships Festival
Bottle Kicking and Hare Pie Scrambling, Hallaton, near Medbourne, Leicestershire
London Marathon
Shakespeare's birthday, Stratford-upon-Avon

May
Furry Dance, Helston, Cornwall
Lancashire Clog Dancing Festival, Accrington
Royal Windsor Horse Show, Windsor Home Park
Chelsea Flower Show, London
Cheese Rolling Festival, Coopers Hill, Gloucestershire

June
Trooping the Colour, Horse Guards Parade, London
Three Counties Show, Malvern, Worcestershire
East of England Show, Peterborough, Cambridgeshire
Wimbledon Tennis Championships
Appleby Horse Fair, Appleby-in-Westmorland, Cumbria
Glastonbury Festival

July
Farnborough International

Airshow, Hampshire
The Great Yorkshire Show, Harrogate
Henley Royal Regatta, Henley-on-Thames, Oxfordshire
Royal International Agricultural Show, Stoneleigh, Warwickshire
Royal International Air Tattoo, Fairford, Gloucestershire

August
International Beatle Week, Liverpool
Rush-bearing ceremony, Grasmere, Cumbria
Southport Flower Show
Billingham International Folklore Festival, Cleveland
Notting Hill Carnival, London
Grasmere Sports, Cumbria
Cowes Regatta, Isle of Wight

September
Blackpool Illuminations
Southampton International Boat Show
Biggest Liar in the World Competition, Santon Bridge, Cumbria
Widecombe Fair, Widecombe-in-the-Moor, Devon

October
Goose Fair, Nottingham
World Conker Championships, Ashton, Northamptonshire

November
Guy Fawkes Night (bonfires and fireworks throughout the country)
London to Brighton Veteran Car Run
Lord Mayor's Show, London

December
Mummers Play and Morris Dancing, Moulton, Northamptonshire

Practical Matters

Above: *Haddon Hall is on e of the best-preserved medieval manor houses in England*
Right: *an attractive hexagonal Victorian letterbox*

TIME DIFFERENCES

GMT
12 noon

British Summer
1PM

Germany
1–2PM

USA (NY)
7AM

Netherlands
1PM

Spain
1PM

BEFORE YOU GO

WHAT YOU NEED

		UK	Germany	USA	Netherlands	Spain
● Required ○ Suggested ▲ Not required	Some countries require a passport to remain valid for a minimum period (usually at least six months) beyond the date of entry – contact their consulate or embassy or your travel agent for details.					
Passport		▲	●	●	●	●
Visa (regulations can change – check before booking your trip)		▲	▲	▲	▲	▲
Onward or Return Ticket		▲	○	○	○	○
Health Inoculations		▲	▲	▲	▲	▲
Health Documentation (➤ 123, Health)		▲	●	●	●	●
Travel Insurance		○	○	○	○	○
Driving Licence (national)		●	●	●	●	●
Car Insurance Certificate (if own car)		▲	●	●	●	●
Car Registration Document (if own car)		▲	●	●	●	●

WHEN TO GO

England

▭ High season
▭ Low season

6°C	7°C	10°C	13°C	17°C	20°C	22°C	22°C	19°C	14°C	10°C	7°C
JAN	FEB	MAR	APR	MAY	JUN	JUL	AUG	SEP	OCT	NOV	DEC
🌧	🌧	🌧	🌦	☀	☀	☀	☀	🌦	🌦	🌧	🌧

🌧 Very wet   🌧 Wet   ☁ Cloud   ☀ Sun   🌦 Sun/Showers

TOURIST OFFICES

In the USA
Suite 701
551 Fifth Avenue
New York
NY 10176
☎ 212/986 2266

Suite 1510
625 N Michigan Ave
Chicago
IL 60611
(personal callers only)

In Canada
Suite 120
5915 Airport Road
Mississauga
L4V 1T7
☎ 905 405 1720
fax: 905 405 8490

POLICE 999

FIRE 999

AMBULANCE 999

WHEN YOU ARE THERE

ARRIVING

There are direct flights to England from all over the world. Most arrive at London Heathrow, Gatwick or Stansted – or Manchester or Birmingham. Ferries serve England from Ireland and many ports in continental Europe. The 24 mile (38km) long Channel Tunnel provides a fast train link with France.

London Heathrow Airport
Kilometres to city centre

25km

Journey times

🚆	60 minutes
🚇	40 minutes
🚌	40 minutes

London Gatwick Airport
Kilometres to city centre

48km

Journey times

🚆	30 minutes
🚌	70–90 minutes
🚌	60–75 minutes

MONEY

Britain's currency is the pound (£), issued in notes of £5, £10, £20 and £50. There are 100 pennies or pence (p) to each pound and coins come in denominations of 1p, 2p, 5p, 10p, 20p, 50p, £1 and £2. Travellers' cheques may be accepted by some hotels, shops and restaurants. Travellers' cheques in pounds are the most convenient.

TIME

 England is on Greenwich Mean Time (GMT) in winter, but from late March until late October British Summer Time (BST, ie GMT+1) operates.

CUSTOMS

 YES
From another EU country for
personal use (guidelines):
3,200 cigarettes, 200 cigars, 3 kilogram of tobacco
10 litres of spirits (over 22%)
20 litres of fortified wine
90 litres of wine, of which 60 litres can be sparkling wine
110 litres of beer

From a non-EU country for your personal use:
200 cigarettes OR
50 cigars OR 250 grams of tobacco
1 litre of spirits (over 22%)
2 litres of fortified wine (e.g. sherry), sparkling wine or other liqueurs
2 litres of still wine
60 ml of perfume
250 ml of eau de toilette

Travellers under 17 years of age are not entitled to the tobacco and alcohol allowances.

 NO
Unlicensed drugs, firearms, ammunition, offensive weapons, obscene material, unlicensed animals, counterfeit and copied goods, meat and poultry.

119

CONSULATES

Germany
0207 824 1300

USA
020 7499 9000

Netherlands
020 7590 3200

Spain
0207 235 5555

WHEN YOU ARE THERE

TOURIST BOARDS

Regional Tourist Boards
Every sizeable town in
England also has a local
tourist information centre.

- Cumbria Tourist Board,
  Ashleigh, Holly Road,
  Windermere, Cumbria
  ☎ 015394 44444

- East of England Tourist
  Board, Toppesfield Hall,
  Hadleigh, Suffolk
  ☎ 01473 822922

- Heart of England Tourist
  Board, Woodside, Larkhill
  Road, Worcester
  ☎ 01905 763436

- London Tourist Board,
  26 Grosvenor Gardens,
  London ☎ 0171 730 3450

- North West Tourist Board,
  Swan House, Swan
  Meadow Road, Wigan
  ☎ 01942 821222

- Northumbria Tourist Board,
  Aykley Heads, Durham
  ☎ 0191 375 3010

- South East England Tourist
  Board, The Old Brew
  House, Warwick Park,
  Tunbridge Wells, Kent
  ☎ 01892 540766

- Southern Tourist Board,
  40 Chamberlayne Road,
  Eastleigh, Hampshire
  ☎ 023 8062 5400

- Southwest Tourist Board,
  Woodwater Park,
  Exeter, Devon ☎ 01392
  360050

- Yorkshire Tourist Board,
  312 Tadcaster Road, York
  YO2 2HF ☎ 01904 707961

NATIONAL HOLIDAYS

J	F	M	A	M	J	J	A	S	O	N	D
1		(1)	(1)	2			1				2

1 Jan	New Year's Day
Mar/Apr	Good Friday, Easter Monday
First Mon in May	May Day Bank Holiday
Last Mon in May	Late May Bank Holiday
Last Mon in August	August Bank Holiday
25 Dec	Christmas Day
26 Dec	Boxing Day

Almost all attractions close on Christmas Day. On
other holidays some attractions open, often with
reduced hours. There are no general rules regarding
the opening times of restaurants and shops, so check
before making a special journey.

OPENING HOURS

○ Shops	● Attractions/museums
● Offices	● Post offices
● Banks	● Pharmacies

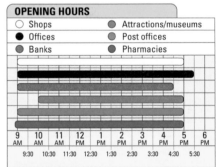

9 AM	10 AM	11 AM	12 PM	1 PM	2 PM	3 PM	4 PM	5 PM	6 PM
9:30	10:30	11:30	12:30	1:30	2:30	3:30	4:30	5:30	

The times shown above are traditional opening hours.
Many shops throughout England, especially those in
the cities and large towns (but increasingly
elsewhere) open for longer hours, many of them now
on Sundays too. High Street banks are generally open
Saturday mornings and bureaux de change are open
daily until late. Many of the museums and visitor
attractions detailed in this guide may close for one
day a week, and often on special occasions. It is
always wise to check the times by telephoning first.
When pharmacies are closed you'll find a sign in the
window giving details of the nearest one that is on 24-
hour duty.

**DRIVE ON THE
LEFT**

**TOILETS
FREE**

PUBLIC TRANSPORT

Internal flights serve the business community, but their often prohibitive cost means that English people rarely use them for 'social' travel. Major British cities – Edinburgh, Glasgow, Cardiff, Belfast – are well served.

Trains All the major towns and cities are connected by fast and frequent services, but intermediate stations tend to be served only by slower services. The lines radiate from London and 'cross-country ' services between provincial cities can be more difficult. The complex nature of the rail system's privatisation in the 1990s means that a variety of differing operators may run trains on the same routes. There is a rail enquiry line to help you plan your journey (08457 484950) and tickets can be bought in advance and over the phone. Tickets are much more expensive if you leave it until your day of travel to buy them.

Buses These come in all shapes and sizes, providing cheap and effective local transport, either in urban areas or connecting small towns and villages in rural areas. Bus companies are privately owned but local authorities often subsidise routes in remote places. A few cities, notably Manchester, Sheffield and Wolverhampton, now run efficient tram services as an alternative to local buses.

Coaches Travel by coach – a long-distance 'bus', and invariably more comfortable – is a slower option than train travel, but its relative cheapness makes it very popular with the budget traveller. Coaches mostly operate under the 'National Express' banner, and serve nearly every town, albeit sometimes infrequently.

CAR RENTAL

The leading international car rental companies have offices at all airports and you can book a car in advance. Local companies offer competitive rates and will deliver a car to the airport .

TAXIS

Anywhere in England you can telephone a private hire company to collect you from where you are and take you to wherever you want to go. Your taxi may be any type of car, though London's famous 'black cabs' are increasingly found in other cities.

DRIVING

Speed limit on motorways and dual carriageways: **70mph (112kph)**

Speed limit on main roads: **50–60mph (80–100kph)**

Speed limit on minor roads: **30–40mph (50–65kph)**

Must be worn in front seats at all times and in rear seats where fitted.

Random breath tests are carried out frequently, especially late at night. The limit is 35 micrograms of alcohol in 100ml of breath.

Fuel is sold in litres and available as unleaded (95 octane), super unleaded (98 octane) and diesel. Other than in the centre of cities, petrol stations are numerous, and many provide basic shopping facilities too. Petrol stations are typically open 6AM–10PM (and 24 hours on major roads) but don't rely on these times in rural areas. Fuel is very heavily taxed, making it more expensive than in Europe or the USA.

If you break down driving your own car and are a member of an AA-affiliated motoring club, you can call the AA (0800 887 766 free phone). If your car is hired, follow the instructions given in the documentation; most rental firms provide a rescue service.

CENTIMETRES

0 1 2 3 4 5 6 7 8

INCHES

0 1 2 3

PERSONAL SAFETY

The cities, towns and villages of England are all generally safe places to be, and policemen are frequently seen walking the beat or patrolling in cars. You will find them friendly, helpful and approachable. You can help minimise the risk of personal crime:

- Don't carry more cash than you need
- Beware of pickpockets in markets and crowded places
- Don't walk alone in dark streets, alleyways or subways

Police assistance:
☎ **999**

from any call box

TELEPHONES

The traditional red phone boxes are now rare; instead, kiosks come in a wide variety of different designs and colours, depending on which phone

company is operating them. Coin-operated telephones take 10p, 20p, 50p and £1 coins, but card-operated phones are often more convenient. Phonecards are available from many shops. Hotel phones are very expensive. To call the operator dial 100.

International Dialling Codes	
From England to:	
Germany:	00 49
USA:	00 1
Canada:	00 1
Netherlands:	00 31
Spain:	00 34

POST

Post offices tend to be open Mon–Fri 9–5:30, Sat 9–1, though there are local variations. Post boxes, which, with few exceptions, are red, come in many shapes and sizes, and provide a fascinating study in themselves. Many date from Victorian times.

ELECTRICITY

The power supply in Britain is 240 volts.
Sockets only accept three

(square)-pin plugs, so an adaptor is needed for Continental and US appliances. A transformer is needed for appliances operating on 110–120 volts.

TIPS/GRATUITIES

Yes ✓ No ✗		
Restaurants (service not included)	✓	10%
Tour Guides	✓	£1–2
Hairdressers	✓	10%
Taxis	✓	10%
Chambermaids (per day)	✓	50p–£1
Porters (depending on number of bags)	✓	50p–£1
Theatre/cinema usher	✗	
Cloakroom attendant	✓	change
Toilets	✗	

Light: England is not renowned for its bright sunshine and the tall buildings create a lot of shadow, so pack plenty of 200 ASA-speed film.

Where you can photograph: Most museums will not allow you to take pictures. Check first.

Where to buy film: As well as specialist camera shops, many high street shops and attractions sell film and camera batteries. Rapid-developing services are also widely available.

HEALTH

Insurance
Nationals of EU and certain other countries can get free medical treatment in Britain with the relevant documentation, although private medical insurance is still advised, and is essential for all other visitors.

 Dental Services
Emergency dental treatment may be available free of charge if you can find a National Health dentist willing to treat you. A list can be found in the Yellow Pages. Dental treatment should be covered by private medical insurance.

Weather
It can rain a lot in England. It can be very sunny too, in July and August, when many of the locals take to the parks to sunbathe. Some sights involve being outdoors for prolonged periods when you should 'cover up', apply sunscreen and drink plenty of water.

 Drugs/Medication
Prescription and non-prescription drugs and medicines are available from chemists/pharmacies. Pharmacists can advise on medication for common ailments. Chemists operate a rota so there will always be one that is open 24 hours; notices in all pharmacy windows give details.

 Safe Water
Tap water is safe to drink. Mineral water is widely available but is often expensive, particularly in restaurants.

CONCESSIONS

Students and Senior Citizens Senior Citizens and holders of an International Student Identity Card will be able to obtain some concessions on travel and entrance fees. There are a handful of good youth hostels in London (➤ 98) and around the country, although you don't have to be young to stay in them.

Children
Concessions for children are usually available when paying for accommodation, travel or admission to an attraction, although there is no consistant age below which a young person is a child!

CLOTHING SIZES

USA	UK	Europe	
36	36	46	Suits
38	38	48	Suits
40	40	50	Suits
42	42	52	Suits
44	44	54	Suits
46	46	56	Suits
8	7	41	Shoes
8.5	7.5	42	Shoes
9.5	8.5	43	Shoes
10.5	9.5	44	Shoes
11.5	10.5	45	Shoes
12	11	46	Shoes
14.5	14.5	37	Shirts
15	15	38	Shirts
15.5	15.5	39/40	Shirts
16	16	41	Shirts
16.5	16.5	42	Shirts
17	17	43	Shirts
6	8	34	Dresses
8	10	36	Dresses
10	12	38	Dresses
12	14	40	Dresses
14	16	42	Dresses
16	18	44	Dresses
6	4.5	38	Shoes
6.5	5	38	Shoes
7	5.5	39	Shoes
7.5	6	39	Shoes
8	6.5	40	Shoes
8.5	7	41	Shoes

WHEN DEPARTING

- Remember to contact the airport on the day before leaving to ensure the flight details are unchanged.
- If travelling by ferry you must check-in no later than the time specified on your ticket.

LANGUAGE

The language spoken by the average English person is a far cry from the 'BBC English' (the kind spoken with perfect clarity and precision on national radio and television news). There are many strong regional accents. Norwich, Liverpool, Birmingham and Newcastle are all places with much idiosyncratic vocabulary. In some areas, the central Pennines, Bristol and Bath for example, accents may change dramatically within the space of a few miles. Don't worry if you don't understand the stronger variant accents, many English people don't either! The impact of greater social mobility and the expansion of metropolitan London into commuterland and 'overspill' towns has tended to blur the distinctions between accents in southeastern England, creating an amorphous linguistic derivative known often called 'Estuarise' or 'Estuary English' after its origins along the Thames estuary. This is certainly more commonly spoken than the Cockney Professor 'Iggins found in the London of *My Fair Lady*. But if you are in London, you can amuse yourself by buying a book on Cockney rhyming slang.

Other regions glory in their distinctive dialects too. You will find humorous translations of the Bible into Yorkshire, jokes in Bristolian, poems in Cumbrian and words of wisdom in the dense brogue of the Black Country district of the West Midlands. The English spoken by the English, even in the BBC, is noticeably different from that spoken by other English speakers in Australia or the USA for example. Below is a list of some of the obvious differences which can be confusing if you're not careful.

❝ Some Anglo-American differences

bill	*restaurant check*	jumble sale	*yard sale*
		jumper	*sweater*
biscuit	*cookie or cracker*	leaflet	*pamphlet*
		lift	*elevator*
bonnet	*car hood*	lorry	*truck*
boot	*car trunk*	motorway	*highway*
caravan	*trailer*	off-licence	*liquor store*
car park	*parking lot*	pavement	*sidewalk*
cheap	*inexpensive*	petrol	*gasoline*
chemist	*pharmacist*	pudding	*dessert*
chips	*french fries*	roundabout	*rotary*
coach	*bus*	road (surface)	*pavement*
crisps	*potato chips*	return ticket	*round trip ticket*
dual carriageway	*divided highway*		
dustbin	*trash can*	single ticket	*one-way ticket*
first floor	*second floor*	subway	*pedestrian passageway*
football	*soccer*		
fortnight	*two weeks*	sweets	*candy*
ground floor	*first floor*	torch	*flashlight*
hire	*rent*	trainers	*sneakers*
jam	*jelly*	underground	*subway*
jelly	*jello*	waistcoat	*vest*

Acknowledgements

The Automobile Association wishes to thank the following photographers and libraries for their assistance in the preparation of this book.

THE ANTHONY BLAKE PHOTO LIBRARY (Neville Kuypers) 9d, (Stephen Read) 50c;
MARY EVANS PICTURE LIBRARY 10b, 11, 14c; **REX FEATURES** 14b, 14d;

The remaining photographs are held in the Association's own library (**AA PHOTO LIBRARY**) and were taken by Derek Forss with the exception of the following: M Allwood-Coppin 60, 62; Adrian Baker 59; Peter Baker 13b, 36b, 43, 49b, 63b, 72c, 76b, 76c, 81, 117a; Jeff Beazley 42c; Malcolm Birkitt 16c; Peter Brown 9c; Ian Burgum 6b; Chris Coe 82, 87, 89; Steve Day 16b, 18b, 20b, 21c, 25b, 46, 65, 67, 69a, 70a, 72a, 75, 76a, 78a; Robert Eames 26b; A J Hopkins 50b, 56b; Caroline Jones 2, 55b, 61, 64b; Max Jourdan 34; S King 21b; Andrew Lawson 18c, 22b; Cameron Lees 12b 19b, 38, 48b; S & O Mathews 6c, 7b, 8b, 68, 85; John Morrison 52; Robert Mort 51b, 90b, 122b; Roger Moss 69b, 71; Rich Newton 15b, 69c, 70b; Michael Short 53, 54a, 55a, 56a, 57a, 64a; Barrie Smith 27a, 28, 29a, 30, 31, 33a, 35a, 35b, 36a; Tony Souter 8c, 88b, 91a; Forbes Stephenson 17b; Rick Strange 9b, 32, 35c, 117b, 122a, 122c; Richard Surman 77; James Tims 51c; Martin Trelawny 91b; Wyn Voysey 5a, 6a, 7a, 8a, 9a, 10a, 10c, 12a, 13a, 14a, 24b, 57b, 72b; Jonathon Welsh 54b; Linda Whitnam 1, 15a, 16a, 17a, 18a, 19a, 20a, 21a, 22a, 23a, 24a, 25a, 26a, 39, 40, 41, 42a, 44a, 44b, 45, 47, 48a, 49a, 50a, 51a, 58, 73, 86b; Harry Williams 74; Tim Woodcock 33b; Gregory Wrona 29b, 37; Jon Wyand 63a

Revised 2003: Isla Love **Managing Editors:** Apostrophe S Limited
Page layout: Nautilus Design (UK) Ltd

Dear Essential Traveller

Your comments, opinions and recommendations are very important to us. So please help us to improve our travel guides by taking a few minutes to complete this simple questionnaire.

You do not need a stamp (unless posted outside the UK). If you do not want to cut this page from your guide, then photocopy it or write your answers on a plain sheet of paper.

Send to: **The Editor, AA World Travel Guides, FREEPOST SCE 4598, Basingstoke RG21 4GY.**

Your recommendations...

We always encourage readers' recommendations for restaurants, nightlife or shopping – if your recommendation is used in the next edition of the guide, we will send you a *FREE* **AA *Essential* Guide** of your choice. Please state below the establishment name, location and your reasons for recommending it.

_____

_____

_____

_____

Please send me **AA *Essential*** _____

(see list of titles inside the front cover)

About this guide...

Which title did you buy?

    AA *Essential* _____

Where did you buy it? _____

When? m m / y y

Why did you choose an AA *Essential* Guide? _____

_____

_____

_____

_____

Did this guide meet your expectations?

    Exceeded ☐   Met all ☐   Met most ☐   Fell below ☐

    Please give your reasons _____

_____

_____

_____

continued on next page...

Were there any aspects of this guide that you particularly liked? ________

____

____

____

Is there anything we could have done better? ________

____

____

____

____

About you...

Name (*Mr/Mrs/Ms*) ________

Address ________

____

________ Postcode ________

Daytime tel nos ________

Which age group are you in?

Under 25 ☐ 25–34 ☐ 35–44 ☐ 45–54 ☐ 55–64 ☐ 65+ ☐

How many trips do you make a year?

Less than one ☐ One ☐ Two ☐ Three or more ☐

Are you an AA member? Yes ☐ No ☐

About your trip...

When did you book? m m / y y When did you travel? m m / y y

How long did you stay? ________

Was it for business or leisure? ________

Did you buy any other travel guides for your trip?

If yes, which ones? ________

____

Thank you for taking the time to complete this questionnaire. Please send it to us as soon as possible, and remember, you do not need a stamp (*unless posted outside the UK*).

Happy Holidays!

The AA and the Automobile Association Limited, their subsidiaries and any other companies or bodies in which either has an interest ('the AA Group') may use information about you to provide you with details of other products and services, by telephone or in writing. The AA Group as a matter of policy does not release its lists to third parties.

If you do not wish to receive further information please tick the box... ☐

The Atlas

Rupert Tenison: detail of Dome of Eden Project

The Automobile Association
www.theAA.com
Offers comprehensive and up-to-the-minute information covering AA-approved hotels, guest houses and B&Bs, restaurants and pubs, along with the latest traffic information and detailed routes to your destination in the UK. Also online access to breakdown cover, car insurance the AA Driving School and Bookshop and much more.

Official England Tourism Website
www.travelengland.org

VisitBritain
Your official travel guide to Britain
www.visitbritain.com

A–Z of England Tourist Sites
www.tourist-boards.com

UK Travel Insurance Directory
www.uktravelinsurancedirectory.co.uk

BBC – Holiday
www.bbc.co.uk/holiday

The Full Universal Currency Converter
www.xe.com/ucc/full.shtml

Flying with Kids
www.flyingwithkids.com

TRAVEL
Flights and Information
www.cheapflights.co.uk
www.thisistravel.co.uk
www.ba.com
www.worldairportguide.com

PUBLIC TRANSPORT
Citylink
www.citylink.co.uk

National Express
www.nationalexpress.com

National Rail Enquiry Service
www.nationalrail.co.uk

Public Transport Information
www.traveline.org.uk

Information about the best fares or buy online
www.thetrainline.com
www.qjump.co.uk

Motorway / Autobahn / Autoroute / Autopista / Autostrada

Motorway toll section / Autobahn gebührenpflichtiger Abschnitt /
Autoroute section à péage / Autopista de pago /
Autostrada tratto a pedaggio

National road, dual carriageway / Zweibhnige Nationalstrasse /
Route nationale à chaussées séparées / Carretera nacional de doble vía /
Strada nazionale a doppia carreggiata

National road, single carriageway / Einbahnige Nationalstrasse /
Route nationale à chaussées unique / Carretera nacional de vía unica /
Strada nazionale a singola carreggiata

Other main road / Haupistrasse / Autre route de liaison principale /
Otra carretera principal / Strada di grande comunicazione

Road numbering: Motorway, other road / Strassennumerierung:
Autobahn, Sonstige Strasse / Numérotation: Autoroute,
Autre route / Numeración de las carreteras: Autopista, Otra carretera /
Numero di strada: Autostrada, Altra strada

Junction / Anschlussstelle / Échangeur / Acceso / Svincolo

Restricted junction / Beschränkte Anschlußstelle / Échangeur partiel /
Acceso parcial / Svincolo con limitazione

Service area / Tankstelle / Aire de service / Área de servicio /
Area di servizio

Internàl boundary / Verwaltungsgrenze / Frontière intérieure /
Límite interno / Confine interno

International airport / Internationaler Flughafen / Aéroport international /
Aeropuerto internacional / Aeroporto internazionale

National park / Nationalpark / Parc national / Parque nacional /
Parco nazionale

Maps © Mairs Geographischer Verlag / Falk Verlag, 73751 Ostfildern

A149

Sheringham
Cromer

A148

North Walsham

Fakenham
Aylsham

A140

A1067

A149

A1151

Dereham

A47

The
Broads

Caister-on-Sea

NORFOLK

Norwich

A47

**Great
Yarmouth**

A1066

A1076

Wymondham

A146

A143

affham

Watton

A11

A143

Lowestoft

Attleborough

A140

A143

Beccles

Bungay

A145

Thetford

A1066

Diss

A144

A1088

A143

Halesworth

Southwold

01

A1120

A12

SUFFOLK

137

A1094

Bury St Edmunds

A134

Stowmarket

A140

A14

D

E

Aldeburgh

F

Woodbridge

TOURIST OFFICES
Regional Tourist Boards

Every sizeable town in England also has a local tourist information centre:

- Cumbria Tourist Board
  Ashleigh, Holly Road, Windermere
  Cumbria ☎ 015394 44444

- East of England Tourist Board
  Toppesfield Hall, Hadleigh
  Suffolk ☎ 01473 822922

- Heart of England Tourist Board
  Woodside, Larkhill Road
  Worcester ☎ 01905 763436

- London Tourist Board
  26 Grosvenor Gardens, London
  ☎ 0171 730 3450

- North West Tourist Board
  Swan House, Swan Meadow Road
  Wigan ☎ 01942 821222

- Northumbria Tourist Board
  Aykley Heads, Durham
  ☎ 0191 375 3010

- South East England Tourist Board
  The Old Brew House, Warwick Park
  Tunbridge Wells, Kent
  ☎ 01892 540766

- Southern Tourist Board
  40 Chamberlayne Road, Eastleigh
  Hampshire ☎ 023 8062 5400

- Southwest Tourist Board
  Woodwater Park, Exeter
  Devon ☎ 01392 360050

- Yorkshire Tourist Board
  312 Tadcaster Road, York
  YO2 2HF ☎ 01904 707961

AA ESSENTIAL Guide
England

It's up to date and easy to use.

Expert travel writer Terry Marsh tells you all you need to know about England.

"Excellent value" *Daily Telegraph*

- The Top 10 sights
- Key places to visit
- Best shopping and nightlife
- Great restaurant choices
- Walks and tours
- 10 don't miss experiences
- Essential fact file
- AND NEW 13 page atlas section – you'll be lost without it

The AA's travel experts have created this guide to help you make the most of your trip. Visit TheAA.com for more AA travel information.

Just **AA** *sk...*

Top 10 Sights

Shopping

Eating Out

Nightlife

Atlas Section

ISBN 0-7495-3951-8

9 780749 539511

£5.99